ARIES

WITCH

♈

© JAMES C. WELCH

Ivo Dominguez, Jr. (**Georgetown, DE**) has been active in the magickal community since 1978. He is one of the founders of Keepers of the Holly Chalice, the first Assembly of the Sacred Wheel coven. He currently serves as one of the Elders in the Assembly. Ivo is the author of several books, including *The Four Elements of the Wise* and *Practical Astrology for Witches and Pagans*. In his mundane life, he has been a computer programmer, the executive director of an AIDS/HIV service organization, a bookstore owner, and many other things. Visit him at www.ivodominguezjr.com.

© SARAH HOOKER PHOTOGRAPHY

Diotima Mantineia (Asheville, NC) is a witch and has been a professional astrologer and tarot reader for more than thirty years. She is also the author of *Touch the Earth, Kiss the Sky: Allowing the Rational Mind to Welcome Magic & Spirituality* (Llewellyn, 2020). She writes for *Witches & Pagans* and teaches widely. Her passion for science led her to a degree in soil and crop science as well as to graduate work in the field. Visit her at http://www.uraniaswell .com.

• UNLOCK THE MAGIC OF YOUR SUN SIGN •

ARIES
WITCH

♈

IVO DOMINGUEZ, JR.
DIOTIMA MANTINEIA

Llewellyn Publications
Woodbury, Minnesota

FIRST EDITION
First Printing, 2023

Art direction and cover design by Shira Atakpu
Book design by Christine Ha
Interior art by the Llewellyn Art Department
Tarot Original 1909 Deck © 2021 with art created by Pamela Colman Smith and Arthur Edward Waite. Used with permission of LoScarabeo.
The Aries Correspondences appendix is excerpted with permission from *Llewellyn's Complete Book of Correspondences: A Comprehensive & Cross-Referenced Resource for Pagans & Wiccans* © 2013 by Sandra Kynes.

Llewellyn Publications is a registered trademark of Llewellyn Worldwide Ltd.

Library of Congress Cataloging-in-Publication Data (Pending)
ISBN: 978-0-7387-7272-1

Llewellyn Worldwide Ltd. does not participate in, endorse, or have any authority or responsibility concerning private business transactions between our authors and the public.

All mail addressed to the author is forwarded but the publisher cannot, unless specifically instructed by the author, give out an address or phone number.

Any internet references contained in this work are current at publication time, but the publisher cannot guarantee that a specific location will continue to be maintained. Please refer to the publisher's website for links to authors' websites and other sources.

Llewellyn Publications
A Division of Llewellyn Worldwide Ltd.
2143 Wooddale Drive
Woodbury, MN 55125-2989
www.llewellyn.com

Printed in the United States of America

Other Books by Ivo Dominguez, Jr.

The Four Elements of the Wise
Keys to Perception: A Practical Guide to Psychic Development
Practical Astrology for Witches and Pagans
Casting Sacred Space
Spirit Speak

Other Books by Diotima Mantineia

Touch the Earth, Kiss the Sky

Other Books in The Witch's Sun Sign Series

Taurus Witch
Gemini Witch
Cancer Witch
Leo Witch
Virgo Witch
Libra Witch
Scorpio Witch
Sagittarius Witch
Capricorn Witch
Aquarius Witch
Pisces Witch

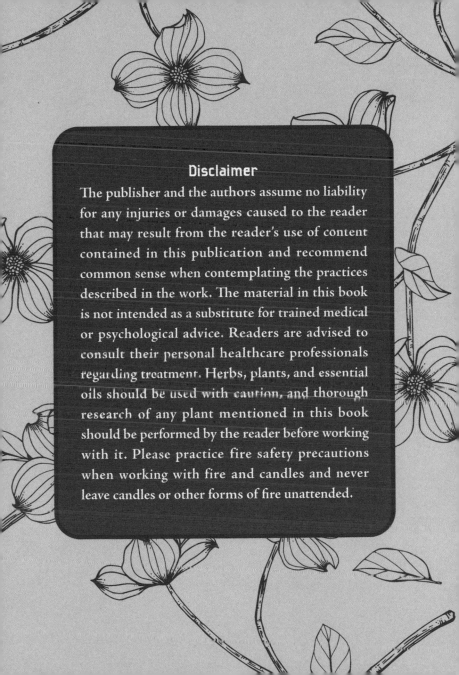

Disclaimer

The publisher and the authors assume no liability for any injuries or damages caused to the reader that may result from the reader's use of content contained in this publication and recommend common sense when contemplating the practices described in the work. The material in this book is not intended as a substitute for trained medical or psychological advice. Readers are advised to consult their personal healthcare professionals regarding treatment. Herbs, plants, and essential oils should be used with caution, and thorough research of any plant mentioned in this book should be performed by the reader before working with it. Please practice fire safety precautions when working with fire and candles and never leave candles or other forms of fire unattended.

CONTENTS

SPELLS, RECIPES, AND PRACTICES

Ivo Dominguez, Jr.

This is the first book in the Witch's Sun Sign series. There are twelve volumes in this series with a book for every Sun sign, but with a special focus on witchcraft. This series explores and honors the gifts, perspectives, and joys of being a witch through the perspective of their Sun sign. Each book has information on how your sign affects your magick and life experiences with insights provided by witches of your Sun sign, as well as spells, rituals, and practices to enrich your witchcraft. This series is geared toward helping witches grow, develop, and integrate the power of their Sun sign into all their practices. Each book in the series has ten writers, so there are many takes on the meaning of being a witch of a particular sign. All the books in the Witch's Sun Sign series are a sampler of possibilities, with pieces that are deep, fun, practical, healing, instructive, revealing, and authentic.

Welcome to the Aries Witch

I'm Ivo Dominguez, Jr., and I've been a witch and an astrologer for over forty years. In this book, and in the whole series, I've written the chapters focused on astrological information and collaborated with the other writers. For the sake of transparency, I am a Sagittarius, and most of the nine other writers for this book are Aries.[1] The chapters focused on the lived experience of being an Aries witch were written by my coauthor, Diotima Mantineia, who has been a professional astrologer, tarot reader, author, and witch for more than thirty years. The spells and shorter pieces written for this book come from a diverse group of strong Aries witches. Their practices will give you a deeper understanding of yourself as an Aries and as a witch. With the information, insights, and methods offered here, your Aries nature and your witchcraft will be better united. The work of becoming fully yourself entails finding, refining, and merging all the parts that make up your life and identity. This all sounds very serious, but the content of this book will run from lighthearted to profound to do justice to the topic. Moreover, this book has practical suggestions on using the power of your Sun sign to improve your craft as a witch. There are many books on Aries or astrology or witchcraft; this book is about wholeheartedly being an Aries witch.

---

1. The exceptions are Dawn Aurora Hunt, who contributes a recipe for each sign in the series, and Sandra Kynes, whose correspondences are listed in the appendix.

There is a vast amount of material available in books, blogs, memes, and videos targeted at Aries. The content presented in these ranges from serious to snarky, and a fair amount of it is less than accurate or useful. After reading this book, you will be better equipped to tell which of these you can take to heart and use, and which are fine for a laugh but not much more. There is a good chance you will be flipping back to reread some chapters to get a better understanding of some of the points being made. This book is meant to be read more than once, and some parts of it may become reference material you will use for years. Consider keeping a folder, digital or paper, for your notes and ideas on being an Aries witch.

What You Will Need

Knowing your Sun sign is enough to get quite a bit out of this book. However, to use all the material in this book, you will need your birth chart to verify your Moon sign and rising sign. In addition to your birth date, you will need the location and the time of your birth as exactly as possible. If you don't know your birth time, try to get a copy of your birth certificate (though not all birth certificates list times). If it is reasonable and you feel comfortable, you can ask family members for information. They may remember an exact time, but even narrowing it down to a range of hours will be useful. There is a solution to not having your exact birth time.

Since it takes moments to create birth charts using software, you can run birth charts that are thirty minutes apart over the span of hours that contains your possible birth times. By reading the chapters that describe the characteristics of Moon signs and rising signs, you can reduce the pile of possible charts to a few contenders. Read the descriptions and find the chart whose combination of Moon sign and rising sign rings true to you. There are more refined techniques a professional astrologer can use to get closer to a chart that is more accurate. However, knowing your Sun sign, Moon sign, and rising sign is all you need for this book. There are numerous websites that offer free basic birth charts you can view online. For a fee, more detailed charts are available on these sites.

You may want to have an astrological wall calendar or an astrological day planner to keep track of the sign and phase of the Moon. You will want to keep track of what your ruling planet, Mars, is doing. Over time as your knowledge grows, you'll probably start looking at where all the planets are, what aspects they are making, and when they are retrograde or direct. You could do this all on an app or a website, but it is often easier to flip through a calendar or planner to see what is going on. Flipping forward and back through the weeks and months ahead can give you a better sense of how to prepare for upcoming celestial influences. Moreover, the calendars and planner contain basic background information about astrology and are a great start for studying astrology.

You're an Aries and So Much More

Every person is unique, complex, and a mixture of traits that can clash, complement, compete, or collaborate with each other. This book focuses on your Aries Sun sign and provides starting points for understanding your Moon sign and rising sign. It cannot answer all your questions or be a perfect fit because of all the other parts that make you an individual. However, you will find more than enough to enrich and deepen your witchcraft as an Aries. There will also be descriptions you won't agree with or you think do not portray you. In some instances, you will be correct, and in other cases, you may come around to acknowledging that the information does apply to you. Astrology can be used for magick, divination, personal development, and more. No matter the purpose, your understanding of astrology will change over time as your life unfolds and your experience and self-knowledge broaden. You will probably return to this book several times as you find opportunities to use more of the insights and methods.

This may seem like strange advice to find in a book for the Aries witch, but remember that you are more than an Aries witch. In the process of claiming the identity of being a witch, it is common to want to have a clear and firm definition of who you are. Sometimes this means overidentifying with a

category, such as fire witch, herb witch, crystal witch, kitchen witch, and so on. It is useful to become aware of the affinities you have so long as you do not limit and bind yourself to being less than you are. The best use for this book is to uncover all the Aries parts of you so you can integrate them well. The finest witches I know have well-developed specialties but also are well rounded in their knowledge and practices.

Onward!

With all that said, the Sun is the starting point for your power and your journey as a witch. The first chapter is about the profound influence your Sun sign has, so don't skip through the table of contents; please start at the beginning. After that, Diotima will dive into magick and practices that come naturally to Aries witches. I'll be walking you through the benefits of picking the right times, places, and things to energize your Aries magick. Diotima will also share a couple of real-life personal stories of her ups and downs, as well as advice on the best ways to protect yourself spiritually and set good boundaries when you really need to. I'll introduce you to how your Moon sign and your rising sign shape your witchcraft. Diotima offers great stories about how her Aries nature comes forward in her life as a witch, and then gives suggestions on self-care and self-awareness. I'll share a full ritual with you to call on the spirit of your sign. Lastly, Diotima offers her wisdom on how to become a better Aries witch. Throughout the whole book, you'll find tables of correspondences, spells, recipes, techniques, and other treasures to add to your practices.

HOW YOUR SUN POWERS YOUR MAGICK

Ivo Dominguez, Jr.

The first bit of astrology people generally learn is their Sun sign. Some enthusiastically embrace the meaning of their Sun sign and apply it to everything in their life. They feel their Sun is shining and all is well in the world. Then at some point, they'll encounter someone who will, with a bit of disdain, enlighten them on the limits of Sun sign astrology. They feel their Sun isn't enough, and they scramble to catch up. What comes next is usually the discovery that they have a Moon sign, a rising sign, and all the rest of the planets in an assortment of signs. Making sense of all this additional information is daunting as it requires quite a bit of learning and/or an astrologer to guide you through the process. Wherever you are on this journey into the world of astrology, at some point you will circle back around and rediscover that the Sun is still in the center.

The Sun in your birth chart shows where life and spirit came into the world to form you. It is the keeper of your spark of spirit and the wellspring of your power. Your Sun is in Aries, so that is the flavor, the color, the type of energy that is at your core. You are your whole birth chart, but it is your Aries Sun that provides the vital force that moves throughout all parts of your life. When you work in harmony and alignment with your Sun, you have access to more life and the capacity to live it better. This is true for all people, but this advice takes on a special meaning for those who are witches. The root of a witch's magick power is revealed by their Sun sign. You can draw on many kinds of energy, but the type of energy you attract with greatest ease is Aries. The more awareness and intention you apply to connecting with and acting as a conduit for that Aries Sun, the more effective you will be as a witch.

The more you learn about the meaning of an Aries Sun, the easier it will be to find ways to make that connection. To be effective in magic, divination, and other categories of workings, it is vital to understand yourself—your motivations, drives, attractions, etc.—so you can refine your intentions, questions, and desired outcomes. Understanding your Sun sign is an important step in that process. One of the goals shared by both witchcraft and astrology is to affirm and to integrate the totality of your nature to live your best life. The glyph for the Sun in astrology is a dot with a circle around it. Your Aries Sun is the dot and the circle, your center, and your circumference. It is your beginning and your journey. It is also the core of your personal Wheel of the Year, the seasons of your life that repeat, have resonances, but are never the same.

How Aries Are You?

The Sun is the hub around which the planets circle. Its gravity pulls the planets to keep them in their courses and bends space-time to create the place we call our solar system. The Sun in your birth chart tugs on every other part of your chart in a similar way. Everything is both bound and free, affected but seeking its own direction. When people encounter descriptions of Aries traits, they will often begin to make a list of which things apply to them and which don't. Some will say they are the epitome of Aries traits, others will claim they are barely Aries, and many will be somewhere in between. Evaluating how closely or not you align with the traditional characteristics of an Aries is not a particularly useful approach to understanding your sign. If you are an Aries, you have all the Aries traits somewhere within you. What varies from person to person is the expression of those traits. Some traits express fully in a classic form, others are blocked from expressing, or are modified, and sometimes there is a reaction to behave as the opposite of what is expected. As an Aries, and especially as a witch, you have the capacity to activate dormant traits, to shape functioning traits, and to tone down overactive traits.

The characteristics and traits of signs are tendencies, drives, and affinities. Gravity encourages a ball to roll down a hill. A plant's leaves will grow in the direction of sunlight. The warmth of a fire will draw people together on a cold night. A flavor you enjoy will entice you to take another bite of your food. Your Aries Sun urges you to be and to act like an Aries. That said, you also have free will and volition to make other choices. Moreover, the rest of your birth chart and the ever-changing celestial influences are also shaping your options, moods, and drives. The more you become aware of the traits and behaviors that come with being an Aries, the easier it will be to choose how you express them. Most people want to have the freedom to make their own choices, but for an Aries, it is doubly important.

As a witch, you have additional tools to work with the Aries energy. You can choose when to access and how you shape the qualities of Aries as they come forth in your life. You can summon the energy of Aries, name the traits you desire, and manifest them. You can also banish or neutralize or ground what you don't need. You can find where your Aries energy short-circuits, where it glitches, and unblock it. You can examine your uncomfortable feelings and your less-than-perfect behaviors to seek the shadowed places within so you can heal or integrate them. Aries is also a spirit and a current of collective consciousness that is vast in size—a group mind and archetype. Aries is not limited to humanity; it engages with plants, animals, minerals, and all the physical and nonphysical beings of the Earth and all its associated realms. As a witch, you can call upon and work with the spiritual entity that is Aries. You can live your life as a ritual. The motion of your life can be a dance to the tune and rhythm of the heavens.

The Aries Glyph

The glyph for Aries is usually described as a simple representation of a ram's horns. That certainly applies, and a charging ram does summarize some Aries behaviors. The glyph can also be interpreted to be a seed sprouting with two leaves burgeoning. Aries is the desire of life to come into being. I often see this glyph as representing a fork in the road. The Aries energy is the energy of freedom, and freedom is about making choices. The Aries glyph is like a simplified drawing of an explosion, an eruption of power coming into the manifest world.

With the use of your imagination, you can see this glyph as a snapshot of the moment of the first outpouring of creation. Recall again the glyph for the Sun: a dot surrounded by a circle. See the dot in your mind's eye. Then see a ray of brilliance spring forth from the dot. Next, the ray splits in two and begins to curl around. The ray leaves the dot behind, and the two segments continue to bend around. The split ray rejoins to become the circle that surrounds the dot.

By meditating on the glyph, you will develop a deeper understanding of what it is to be an Aries. You may also come up with your own personal gnosis or story about the glyph that can be a key that is uniquely yours. The glyph for Aries can be used as a sigil to call or concentrate its power. The glyph for Aries can be used in a similar fashion to the scribing of an invoking pentacle that is used to open the gates to the elemental realms. However, instead of the elemental realms, this glyph opens the way to the realm of mind and spirit that is the source of Aries. To make this glyph work for you, you need to deeply ingrain the feeling of scribing this glyph. Visually, it is a simple glyph, so memorizing it is easy, but having a kinesthetic feel for it turns it into magick. Spend some time doodling the glyph on paper. Try drawing the glyph on your palm with a finger for several repetitions as that adds several layers of sensation and memory patterns.

Whenever you need access to more magical energy, confidence, centering, and so on, scribe the Aries glyph in your mind, on your hand, in the air, however you can. Then pull and channel and feel your center fill with whatever you need. It takes very little time to open this connection using the glyph. Consider making this one of the practices you use to get ready to do divination, spell work, ritual, or just to start your day.

Aries Patterns

This is a short list of patterns, guidelines, and predilections for Aries Sun people to get you started. If you keep a book of shadows, or a journal, or files on a digital device to record your thoughts and insights on magickal work, you may wish to create your own list to expand upon these. The process of observing, summarizing, and writing down your own ideas in a list is a great way to learn about your sign.

🔥 Aries is drawn to the roles of warrior, pathfinder, and pioneer.

🔥 Jumping headlong into action is the default for Aries.

🔥 Although their behaviors read as strong-willed, confident, and self-possessed, Aries needs to be reassured by others that they are brave and strong.

🔥 Aries can swiftly swing from being assertive to being aggressive. Be clear on the what and the why of your deeds, and whether the outcomes match your intentions.

🔥 When you have a cause to pursue or a heart's desire, you tap into a tremendous current of energy that renews itself quickly.

🔥 When you are at your best, your actions are inspirational to others. When you are not acting from your better nature, others can feel bullied or erased.

🔥 Aries has the gift of pure existence—the power to be, and to revel in simply being themselves.

🔥 Aries loves to laugh, and they know how to let others in on the joke. This is the balm that soothes the excess fire that sometimes burns those near to you.

🔥 Your desire to take charge, to set things right, and to protect those around you is both a blessing and a challenge.

🔥 Fiery passions come easily to an Aries, but connecting with their cooler emotions and deeper feelings requires conscious choice to develop. It is well worth the work, for an Aries in touch with their heart can accomplish almost anything.

- 🔥 Learn to walk away from a fight and only agree to battles worthy of your interest.

- 🔥 If you don't feel passionate about something, it is not your work nor your calling. If there is something tedious you must do to reach your goals, view it as a challenge to surmount, and you will have the drive you need.

- 🔥 Impatience or boredom are warning signs that you need to find something to do. If you don't, the energy will build and burst forth in ways that are not productive.

- 🔥 When you are irritated by someone's complaints or whining, pay close attention, as there is probably a useful piece of information or a lesson to be found.

- 🔥 Aries are happiest when they live their lives like an open book.

- 🔥 The world does need more people willing to save the day and fight the good fight, and an Aries is often among the first to answer the call. Try not to rush so much that you leave without getting the details, and always have a backup plan.

🔥 For an Aries, there is no such thing as having too much energy. The trick is in finding ways to put it to good use.

🔥 Honesty is important to you, and so are first impressions. Pretend that every time you meet someone, it is the first time again, even if it is the tenth. This way, you can become a better judge of character.

🔥 Anger can come to you strongly and suddenly, but you let go of it just as quickly, which is a gift. Be mindful that others may be affected by your anger when it is little more than a fading memory for you.

🔥 In some spiritual systems, the importance of letting go of the ego in favor of its dissolution or merger with a higher consciousness is seen as a paramount goal. For Aries, their life work is about proving and improving themselves, and the same applies to their egos. Polish the jewel of your ego and executive function; don't cast it away.

Cardinal Fire

The four elements come in sets of three. The modalities known as cardinal, fixed, and mutable are three different flavors or styles of manifestation for the elements. The twelvefold pattern that is the backbone of astrology comes from the twelve combinations produced from four elements times three modalities. As you go around the wheel of the zodiac,  the order of the elements is always fire, earth, air, then water, while the modalities are always in the order of cardinal, fixed, then mutable. Each season begins in the cardinal modality, reaches its peak in the fixed modality, and transforms to the next season in the mutable modality. The cardinal modality is the energy of creation bursting forth, coming into being, and spreading throughout the world. The fixed modality is the harmonization of energy so that it becomes and remains fully itself and is preserved. Fixed does not mean static or passive; it is the work of maintaining creation. The mutable modality is the energy of flux that is flexibility, transformation, death, and rebirth.

Aries is the first sign in the zodiac, so it is fire of the cardinal modality. This is why an Aries witch can call up power and passion so quickly. Although as an Aries witch you can call upon fire in all its forms, it is easiest to draw upon cardinal fire.

The elements and modalities on the wheel

Mars, Your Ruling Planet

Your Sun sign determines the source and the type of energy you have in your core. The ruling planet for a sign reveals your go-to moves and your intuitive or habitual responses for expressing that energy. Your ruling planet provides a curated set of prebuilt responses and custom-tailored stances for you to use in day-to-day life. Mars is the ruling planet for Aries. The first association that springs to mind for many on hearing the name Mars is the Roman god of war. However, the planet Mars and how it influences Aries is more complicated, and the martial qualities are just a fraction of what it brings. Mars is assertive and protective behavior, not just aggressive behavior. Mars is also the root of passion, especially sexual passion. Mars is all forms of physical vitality, vigor, and health itself. Mars is the force that moves in all that lives. Mars shows itself equally well in the charging ram, the puppy zooming around a yard, or a kitten rocketing around your home. Mars asks you to leap into action, trust your intuition, trust your training, and figure it out as you go. It is no wonder that Aries is known for rushing headfirst into challenges and adventures.

Aries witches are more strongly affected by whatever Mars is doing in the heavens. It is useful to keep track of the aspects Mars is making with other planets. You can get basic information on what aspects mean and when they are happening in astrological calendars and online resources. You will feel Mars retrogrades more strongly than most people. Aries witches will notice that the impact of the Mars retrograde will start earlier and end a few days later than the listed duration. Also, when Mars in the heavens is in Aries, you will feel an extra boost of energy. This first step to using the power of Mars is to pay attention to what it is doing, how you feel, and what is happening in your life. Witches can shift their relationship with the powers that influence them. Awareness makes it possible to harness those energies to purposes you choose. Close your eyes, feel for that power, and channel it into your magick.

Mars can be as great a source of energy for an Aries witch as the element of fire. Although there is some overlap between the qualities and capacities assigned to Mars and fire, the differences are greater. Mars rules how you are competitive. Fire shapes what you desire. Mars has the power to destroy. Fire has the power to purify. Mars revels in consumption and acquisition. Fire revels in transformation and creation. Mars thwarted turns inward and becomes anger or depression. Fire thwarted burns hotter and blazes forth into places where it should not. Over time, you can map out the overlapping regions and the differences between Mars and fire. Using both planetary and elemental resources can give you a much broader range and more finesse.

Aries and the Zodiacal Wheel

The order of the signs in the zodiac can also be seen as a creation story. The first third of the zodiac is the first appearance of the four elements in the story of the universe. They are fresh from the maelstrom of creation; they are closest to the source. Aries remembers the moment of creation. The fire of Aries is the most primal of all the versions of the element of fire. Although Aries is sometimes stereotyped as impulsive and perhaps reckless, their primal fire is also pure and has faith in their power. Although true for all witches, the Aries witch needs to apply themselves to discovering who they are and where their power dwells within them. When you can consistently connect with that spark that is your most authentic self, you become the geyser of fire that can energize anything. You can make progress in this quest through meditation and inner journeys, but that alone will not do. The Aries witch learns by doing; action is the greatest teacher. When an Aries witch connects to the spiritual qualities of their fire, they become a warrior, life's torchbearer, and are excited about following their path, come what may.

The sign and planet rulers on zodiac wheel

ARIES
CORRESPONDENCES

Power: To Be

Keyword: Vitality

Roles: Warrior, Pioneer, Explorer

Ruling Planet: Mars

Element: Cardinal Fire

Colors: Red, Scarlet, White

Shape: Pentagon

Metals: Iron and Steel

Body Part Ruled: The Head

Day of the Week: Tuesday

Affirmation:
*In following my initiative,
I become myself.*

WITCHCRAFT THAT COMES NATURALLY TO AN ARIES

Diotima Mantineia

As the first sign of the zodiac, Aries is associated with birth and beginnings, and the first beginning we experience in this life is the birth of our soul into a physical body. Fire is Aries' element, and, on an esoteric level, fire is known as the gateway between the world of spirit and the physical realm. Fire comes naturally to the Aries witch. We are in our element when we are working with either physical fire or more esoteric manifestations of fire, such as our cellular metabolism and the life force that animates our subtle body.

There are so many ways to work with fire—some of my favorites are dancing around a bonfire and candle magic. I also practice inner fire meditations that build subtle energy through breath practices (remember that air feeds fire). Fire scrying is something I wish I was better at, because I love sitting around a fire outdoors in the summer and in front of my fireplace in the winter.

But it's important to be careful. Fire—much like the famous Aries temper—can get out of hand quickly. Never neglect safety precautions.

To really get a feel for the element of fire, it helps to know something about its physical properties. The four classical elements are directly related to the four states of matter in chemistry: gas (air), liquid (water), solid (earth), and plasma (fire). Plasma is the only state of matter in which the atoms are stripped of their electrons, forming an electrically charged gas, which manifests not only as fire, but as the bright light of neon signs, the stunning Northern Lights—the aurora—and the hot core of stars as well.

This electrically charged, fluid state of energy is one we can easily tap into to restore our personal energy or gather power for our magic. I like to quickly pass a talisman through or near a flame and imagine the dancing, free electrons of the flame surrounding and enlivening it with their considerable energy. If I lived where the Northern Lights are seen, I'd definitely leave magical objects out to be charged on the nights they manifest.

Connecting with the Spirit World

Across many religions and cultures, fire is seen as a gateway between the physical realm and the realm of the ancestors, the realm of spirit. As the firstborn of fire in the zodiac, Aries maintains a close connection with the spirit world. That connection makes working in trance to contact deities, ancestors, or other spirits a natural talent for most of us (though certain other planetary placements, such as a strong Saturn or Moon in an Earth sign, might work to make that talent a bit harder to access for some of us).

I began working with trance states in the mid-1980s, and this work opened up a whole new world to me. It took me a while to deal with the existential doubts and self-questioning that were the result of my years of scientific training and my naturally skeptical Aquarius Moon, but my undeniable experiences in trance eventually got me over the obstacles.

Fire signs are naturally intuitive, and Aries is no exception. Most of us will find it easy to access trance states, though our primary focus remains on the physical world. The existential challenge of birth—making a place for ourselves in this world—will always be what drives an Aries. But trance states can help us understand more about how to create within physical reality and keep us connected to the unlimited energy that comes from the spirit realm, to the knowledge and magical power that is available to us there.

However, there is a caveat. Aries tend to rush in where the proverbial angels fear to tread, and we can get ourselves in trouble if we don't bother to learn the skills and techniques of trance work. Taking the time to learn how to do it safely first helps us avoid problematic situations and spirits and find our way back to our normal level of consciousness.

An Aries witch's favorite ways of accessing trance usually involve motion, like dancing (particularly around a bonfire!) or walking a labyrinth. Even if we are sitting down, swaying, moving our hands, shaking a rattle, or beating a drum can help us access a trance state.

Magic

But movement isn't only an effective way of entering trance. Movement also helps raise magical energy for spells. Magical techniques that utilize anything from hand gestures to full-body movement are not only a natural talent for Aries, but also help keep us from getting (gods forbid!) bored. Keeping our magic powerful means keeping our magic fresh.

A bored Aries is magically compromised, and we are easily bored. Magic that involves a lot of repetition generally doesn't appeal to us. What we want is fun, passion, and inspiration. It helps to switch things up magically when we aren't feeling inspired. For instance, when I began writing my sections of this book, I was going to charge a candle for the whole book and burn it as I wrote. But what came to hand as I was rooting through my basket of candles was a bunch of glittery, white, tall birthday candles, and I was drawn to use them. Reaching in again, the next box I grabbed was more birthday candles—these were spiral-shaped, with a metallic sheen and different colors.

Then I realized that I didn't need a candle for the whole book—I had no doubt that Ivo, my coauthor, had the magic for that well in hand. What I wanted was the fun of working with candles of whatever color currently appealed to me, anointing them with different oils or potions, charging a new one to light that spark of inspiration in me every time I sat down to write.

This is why birthday candles are great for Aries candle magic. While we may develop the discipline and patience to work long-term spells when needed, the impatient Aries soul often wants to work a spell fast, or a bunch of short spells in sequence, and birthday candles are perfect for that. So, my sections of this book were magically inspired and supported by a rainbow of different colored birthday candles.

Another type of magic that comes naturally to Aries is called "road opening" in the African American magical traditions of hoodoo. It's a magical working that not only removes blockages but creates opportunities for progress. Aries is a pioneering spirit and loves to find new paths and new ways to move forward.

While working with hoodoo requires some specific training, you can develop your own path-clearing/opportunity-drawing spells. In fact, Aries witches love inventing new spells! If you are experienced in spell work, you'll be able to invent a working using techniques in your own magical tradition.

A Spell for Clearing a Path

By Diotima Mantinea

If you are still relatively new at magic, here's a template spell you can use to get started. Feel free to improvise as you gain more knowledge and experience. Just recognize that, as with cooking, experience helps you learn what in a recipe can be changed or adjusted, and what can't. If you're not sure, ask someone with more experience, or stick with the recipe.

You will need:

+ A 4" x 4" piece of paper

+ A pen

+ A yellow or orange candle that is small enough to burn completely in the time you have available for the spell

+ A sturdy holder for the candle

+ A bit of plain olive oil, with a drop or two of lavender and/or lemongrass essential oil added (the essential oils are optional)

+ Incense (lavender, cedar, or any Mercury incense)

+ A fireproof dish big enough to burn the paper

34

Instructions:

You can do this spell at any time, but ideally under a waxing Moon in either Gemini or Sagittarius. Read through this spell first, then prepare the materials and put them on your altar.

First, a bit of meditation is in order. Where do you feel stuck and like you can't see the way forward? In what area of your life do you want new perspectives and new opportunities to arise? Write these thoughts down so you are clear on what you want this spell to do.

Now go sit at your altar and do whatever you normally would to prepare yourself for magic. If you work with your ancestors, any helping spirits, or deities, ask them to be with you now. Or just call to your higher/greater Self.

State your intention clearly. Say something like, "I come here today to clear a path ahead in my [area of life], and to draw new and beneficial opportunities to me." Light the incense.

Pick up the dish with the oil, hold it between your palms, and say something like, "I bless this oil to my purpose of opening a path ahead in my [area of life]." Pick up the candle, anoint it with the oil, and say, "I charge this candle to my purpose of opening a path ahead in my [area of life]." Put the candle in the holder.

Now write the following (or something like it) on the paper:

The path to a better [area of life] *opens before me*
New opportunities beckon me forward
Luck walks with me as I travel into my bright future

Sign your name, then speak the written words out loud. Fold the paper toward you once, then turn it 90 degrees, and fold it toward you again. Put it under the candle holder. Light the candle. When the candle is almost completely gone, but still lit, remove the paper from under the candle and light it in the flame. Drop it into the fireproof dish, and let it burn to ash. When the candle has burned out, take the ash from the paper outside, and fling or blow the ash into the air. Say, "It is done."

Divination

Given our impulsive nature, it's helpful for the Aries witch to develop divination skills. When we get an impulse to do something where the outcome will have a real impact on our lives, taking a few minutes to consider how that might work out for us is usually a good idea, and divination can help with that.

No matter what style of divination you use, have a ritual you perform first. While an Aries witch can be very focused when we choose to, we often need some help to get into that focused state. The ritual I developed when I was first learning tarot involves touching three specific spots on my body, repeating a brief invocation, and lighting a candle. Initially, I did a full ritual to clearly connect those gestures and words to specific states of mind, and to the spirits who assist me with divination. Now that everything is connected, the process takes about thirty seconds. I have a slightly different ritual I use before an appointment with an astrology client.

Create a ritual that works for you. This can be very simple: a special breathing pattern, a gesture you would not normally make, perhaps lighting a candle, done with the intention of connecting you to spiritual guidance. Do a full ritual at least once, calling in whatever guidance you connect with when you divine and repeating the actions several times. This will establish the ritual firmly in your mind and muscle memory. You'll also want to develop a similar brief ritual of disconnecting from that psychic space once you are done.

Use these rituals every time you divine, both to improve your divinations and to protect your own energetic/psychic boundaries.

Ritual

Taking action is important to Aries. We want to *do* things— anything that affects or changes the world around us. And we tend to not spend a lot of time thinking before we act. This is why ritual is so useful for the Aries witch—it allows us to take action toward a goal, but it requires us to do some thinking first. Often, we can get impatient with the demands of ritual—planning, setup, timing—but these demands help us focus our often-scattered energy and clarify our intentions.

While we can do rituals solo, we benefit from group rituals, and we have a lot of energy to contribute to them. Once that ritual energy starts flowing, the Aries witch will take it and move it right along. We're very good at moving energy, but in group rituals, it's important for us to pay attention to how our energy is blending with the overall group energy.

Autonomy is important to the Aries witch, and if we find ourselves in a group situation, we usually prefer to be the ones leading the group and calling the shots. Out in front of the crowd is where we feel most comfortable. But the comfortable place is not always the best place.

Working within a coven or participating in group rituals helps us see the perspectives of others. We learn the power of individuals working magic together, as well as how a true leader always puts the needs of the group first. Leadership is a life lesson for Aries.

Still, many of us prefer to work our magic solo, and get our leadership lessons in other arenas of our lives. The practice of witchcraft is malleable, and the Aries witch takes full advantage of that. Even if we are working with groups, our individual practices are important to us because Aries are here to explore what it means to be a sovereign individual, and witchcraft is an unparalleled method for doing that.

MAGICAL
CORRESPONDENCES

♈

You'll find certain types of spells and magical workings are perfect for an Aries. Here are some suggestions for the types of spells you're likely to resonate with, magical tools that are a good fit for our magic, and some thoughts on magical goals and ideas for spells.

Types of Spellcraft

- Candle magic
- Fire dancing
- Road opening
- Fire purification
- Trance work
- Fire scrying

Magical Tools

+ Wand
+ Sword
+ Boline (*crescent-shaped knife*)
+ Flint and steel
+ Lanterns
+ Candles

Magical Goals and Spell Ideas

+ Protection and banishing magic
+ Spells to bring victory
+ Start-up magic to get a project off the ground
+ Courage and confidence spells
+ Healing that recharges vitality
+ Spells for clarity of purpose

TIMING, PLACES, AND THINGS

Ivo Dominguez, Jr.

You've probably encountered plenty of charts and lists in books and online, cataloging which things relate to your Sun sign and ruling planet. There are many gorgeously curated assortments of herbs, crystals, music playlists, fashions, sports, fictional characters, tarot cards, and more that are assigned to your Sun sign. These compilations of associations are more than a curiosity or for entertainment. Correspondences are like treasure maps to show you where to find the type and flavor of power you are seeking. Correspondences are flowcharts and diagrams that show the inner occult relationship between subtle energies and the physical world. Although there are many purposes for lists of correspondences, there are two that are especially valuable to becoming a better Aries witch.

The first is to contemplate the meaning of the correspondences, the ways in which they reveal meaningful details about your Sun sign and ruling planet, and how they connect to you. This will deepen your understanding of what it is to be an Aries witch.

The second is to use these items as points of connection to access energies and essences that support your witchcraft. This will expand the number of tools and resources at your disposal for all your efforts.

Each of the sections in this chapter will introduce you to a type of correlation with suggestions on how to identify and use it. These are just starting points, and you will find many more as you explore and learn. As you broaden your knowledge, you may find yourself a little bit confused as you find that sources disagree on the correlations. These contradictions are generally not a matter of who is in error but a matter of perspective, cultural differences, and the intended uses for the correlations. Anything that exists in the physical world can be described as a mixture of all the elements, planets, and signs. You may be an Aries, but depending on the rest of your chart, there may be strong concentrations of other signs and elements. For example, if you find that a particular herb is listed as associated with both Aries and Scorpio, it is because it contains both natures in abundance. In the cases of strong multiple correlations, it is important to summon or tune in to the one you need.

Times

You always have access to your power as an Aries witch, but there are times when the flow is stronger, readily available, or more easily summoned. There are sophisticated astrological methods to select dates and times that are specific to your birth chart. Unless you want to learn quite a bit more astrology or hire someone to determine these for you, you can do quite well with simpler methods. Let's look at the cycles of the solar year, the lunar month, and the hours of day-night rotation. When the Sun is in Aries, or the Moon is in Aries, or for the hour or so starting at dawn every day, you are in the sweet spot for tuning in to the core of your power.

The Sun enters Aries at the spring equinox in the northern hemisphere. The date for the spring equinox varies because the calendar is not anchored to celestial events. Aries season is roughly March 21–April 19, but check your astrological calendar or ephemeris to determine when it is for a specific year. The amount of energy that is accessible is highest when the Sun is at the same degree of Aries as it is in your birth chart. This peak will not always be on your birth date, but very close to it. Take advantage of Aries season for working magic and for recharging and storing up energy for the whole year.

The Moon moves through the twelve signs every lunar cycle and spends around two and half days in each sign. When the Moon is in Aries, you have access to more lunar power because the Moon in the heavens has a resonant link to the Sun in your birth chart. At some point during its time in Aries, the Moon will be at the same degree as your Sun. For you, that will be the peak of the energy during the Moon's passage through Aries that month. While the Moon is in Aries, your psychism is stronger, as is your ability to manifest things. When the Moon is in its first quarter, in any sign, you can draw upon its power more readily because that phase is about growth and action.

Aries is the first sign in the order of the zodiac and is associated with not only the northern spring equinox, but also with the dawn and the rising of the Sun. Every morning at sunrise, there is a symbolic linkage with the cardinal fire of Aries. The first hour is the most powerful, but the closer you get to the actual moment of sunrise, the better. The power that flows during this time is more the primal fires of Aries than its other qualities. Plan on using the power of dawn for fire magic, purification, getting out of a rut, and strengthening your will and passions.

The effect of these special times can be joined in any combination. For example, you can choose to do work at dawn when the Moon is in Aries, or when the Sun is in Aries at dawn, or when the Moon is in Aries during Aries season. You can combine all three as well. Each time period grouping will have a distinctive feeling. Experiment and use your instincts to discover how to use these in your work.

Places

There are activities, professions, phenomena, and behaviors that have an affinity, a resonant connection, to Aries and its ruling planet, Mars. These activities occur in the locations that suit or facilitate their expressions. There is magic to be claimed from those places that is earmarked for Aries or your ruling planet of Mars. Just like your birth chart, the world around contains the influences of all the planets and signs, but in different proportions and arrangements. You can always draw upon Aries or Mars energy, but places and spaces have energies that accumulate and can be tapped as well. Places contain the physical, emotional, and spiritual environments that are created by the actions of the material objects, plants, animals, and people occupying those spaces. Some of the interactions between these things can generate or concentrate the energies and patterns that can be used by Aries witches.

If you look at traditional astrology books, you'll find listings of places assigned to Aries and Mars that include locations such as these:

 Sports venues and gyms

 Military bases, police stations, and battlefields

 Landscapes with rough terrain or arid places

These are very clearly linked to the themes associated with Aries and Mars. With a bit of brainstorming and free-associating, you'll find many other less obvious locations and situations where you can draw upon this power. For example, high-energy or aggressive music at a concert produces a current you can plug into. Any competitive activity, whether it is a chess tournament, a dance-off, or gaming on an app, can become a source of power for an Aries witch. All implements or actions that cut, puncture, or cleave are correlated to Mars, so a plow cutting through the soil, an artisan carving wood, a surgeon at work, people having a lively debate, and many more settings also could be a source for energy.

While you can certainly go to places that are identified as locations where Aries and/or Mars energy is plentiful to do workings, you can find those energies in many other situations. Don't be limited by the idea that the places must be the ones that have a formalized link to Aries. Be on the lookout for Aries or Mars themes and activities wherever you may be. Remember that people thinking, feeling, or participating in activities connected to your sign and its ruling planet are raising power. If you can identify with it as resonating with your Sun sign or ruling planet, then you can call the power and put it to use. You complete the circuit to engage the flow with your visualization, intentions, and actions.

Plants

Aries is fiery, active, sharp edged, and its color is every hue of red. Mars overlaps with these, but also adds a focus on blood flow, more heat, and qualities that cause or relieve inflammation. Herbs, resins, oils, fruits, vegetables, woods, and flowers that strongly exhibit one or more of these qualities can be called upon to support your magic. Here are a few examples:

- 🔥 Cayenne or other hot peppers because they produce heat, are piquant, and are often red.

- 🔥 Ginger because it warms the body, aids blood flow, and stokes the fire of digestion.

- 🔥 Dragon's Blood resin in incense because of its red color and the intensity of its energy.

- 🔥 Coffee and guarana because they stimulate activity and make the blood race.

- 🔥 Rue and other cleansing or antimicrobial herbs because they have a warrior nature.

Once you understand the rationale for making these assignments, the lists of correspondences will make more sense. Another thing to consider is that each part of a plant may resonate more strongly with a different element, planet, and sign. The thorns, prickly parts, and spines of a plant may relate to Aries and Mars while other parts of the plant belong to another combination of celestial influences. A thorny red rose is as much linked to Aries and Mars as it is to Taurus and Venus. Which energy steps forward depends on your call and invitation. Like calls to like is a truism in witchcraft. When you use your Aries nature to make a call, you are answered by the Aries part of the plant.

Plant materials can take the form of incense, anointing oils, altar pieces, potions, washes, magickal implements, foods, flower arrangements, and so on. The mere presence of plant material that is linked to Aries or Mars will be helpful to you. However, to gain the most benefit from plant energy, you need to actively engage with it. Push some of your energy into the plants and then pull on it to start the flow. Although much of the plant material you work with will be dried or preserved, it retains a connection to living members of their species. You may also want to reach out and try to commune with the spirit, the group soul, of the plants to request their assistance or guidance. This will awaken the power slumbering in the dried or preserved plant material. Spending time with living plants, whether they be houseplants, in your yard, or in a public garden, will strengthen your connection to the green fire of Aries.

Crystals and Stones

Before digging into this topic, let's clear up some of the confusion around the birthstones for the signs of the zodiac. There are many varying lists for birthstones. Also be aware that some are related to the calendar month rather than the zodiacal signs. There are traditional lists, but the most commonly available lists for birthstones were created by jewelers to sell more jewelry. Also be cautious of the word *traditional* as some jewelers refer to the older lists compiled by jewelers as "traditional." The traditional lists created by magickal practitioners also diverge from each other because of cultural differences and the availability of different stones in the times and places the lists were created. If you have already formed a strong connection to a birthstone that you discover is not really connected to the energy of your sign, keep using it. Your connection is proof of its value to you in moving, holding, and shifting energy, whether or not it is specifically attuned to Aries.

These are my preferred assignments of birthstones for the signs of the zodiac:

Aries	Bloodstone, Carnelian, Diamond
Taurus	Rose Quartz, Amber, Sapphire
Gemini	Agate, Tiger's Eyes, Citrine
Cancer	Moonstone, Pearl, Emerald
Leo	Heliodor, Peridot, Black Onyx
Virgo	Green Aventurine, Moss Agate, Zircon
Libra	Jade, Lapis Lazuli, Labradorite
Scorpio	Obsidian, Pale Beryl, Nuummite
Sagittarius	Turquoise, Blue Topaz, Iolite
Capricorn	Black Tourmaline, Howlite, Ruby
Aquarius	Amethyst, Sugalite, Garnet
Pisces	Ametrine, Smoky Quartz, Aquamarine

There are many other possibilities that work just as well, and I suggest you find what responds best for you as an individual. I've included all twelve signs in case you'd like to use the stones for your Moon sign or rising sign. Hands-on experimentation is the best approach, so I suggest visiting crystal or metaphysical shops and rock and mineral shows when possible. Here's some information on the three I prefer for Aries:

Bloodstone

Bloodstone encourages persistence by giving clarity of direction; it increases physical and spiritual vitality and helps to remove blockages in your energy. It helps calm impatience and irritation when dealing with unexpected situations or troublesome people. Bloodstone also helps cleanse the blood and promotes the release of toxins or toxic energy. It helps restore your courage and self-confidence when you have over-extended yourself. This crystal also acts as a bridge to connect you with the energies of other crystals, people, plants, and spirits. This is useful in various kinds of workings. It also can make it easier to ground or release excess energy by anchoring you in the greater flow of life around you.

Carnelian

Carnelian increases your capacity to take in power. It also helps to stabilize your emotions and protects you from some of the hazards of working at or just above the limits of your capacity. To a lesser degree, it also helps keep you grounded and your head clear while you are working. A single large stone is more effective than multiple small stones. The brighter the color, the stronger the impact of the carnelian for this purpose. It need not be touching the skin to be effective. However, it must be no more than a hand's width away from your skin to be close enough to function well.

Diamond

Diamonds almost didn't make my list because the mining of diamonds is historically linked with serious human rights violations and disregard for the pollution caused by their mining. However, there are many diamonds already in circulation that have been passed as family heirlooms, gifts, and so on that you may already own. If you want to buy a diamond, there are now diamond mines that have begun to operate under guidelines to ensure fair pay and good treatment of workers and respect for the environment. Ask questions before you buy diamonds.

So why are diamonds given all those concerns?

Diamonds are made of carbon, the element that anchors all life on Earth. Diamonds are the hardest natural material and the crystal that conducts heat best. It can focus and channel a remarkable amount of energy without resistance. It can amplify whatever is sent into it. Diamonds can be used to strengthen shields and wards. They remind you that your core is invincible.

Intuition and spiritual guidance play a part in the making of correlations and, in the case of traditional lore, the collective experience of many generations of practitioners. There is also reasoning behind how these assignments are made, and understanding the process will help you choose well. In addition to the stones correlated to Aries, stones that are the opposite of the themes associated with Aries are helpful. In those cases, the logic is about providing a counterbalance or smoothing out an excessive manifestation of Aries or Mars traits. Here are some examples of this reasoning (most red crystals have an alignment with Aries and Mars):

🔥 The metal that is assigned to Aries is iron. Consequently, crystals that have significant amounts of iron, such as hematite, pyrite, and tiger iron, are correlated.

🔥 Crystals whose lore and uses are related to Aries or Mars actions or topics, such as physical vitality and confidence, are recommended as crystals for Aries, such as sunstone, citrine, and red jasper.

🔥 Amethyst or sodalite appear on lists of crystals for Aries because they help cool down impulsive behavior and overheated agitation.

The crystals suggested for Libra, your opposite sign, are also useful to maintain your balance, such as jade, lapis lazuli, and labradorite.

Ritual Objects and the Aries Witch

A substantial number of traditions or schools of witchcraft use magickal tools that are consecrated to represent and hold the power of the elements. Oftentimes in these systems, there is one primary tool for each of the elements. Some correlate fire to the staff and some to the sword, and they all work within their own context. Find and follow what works best for you.

Magickal tools and ritual objects are typically cleansed, consecrated, and charged to prepare them for use. In addition to following whatever procedure you may have for preparing your tools, add in a step to incorporate your energy and identity as an Aries witch. This is especially productive for magickal tools and ritual objects that are connected to fire or are used for protective work or the setting of boundaries. By adding Aries energy and patterning into the preparation of your tools, you will find it easier to raise, move, and shape energy with them in your workings.

There are many magickal tools and ritual objects that need not be element specific. These tools in particular benefit from being filled with Aries energy to make them more responsive to your intentions.

A Charging Practice

When you consciously use your Aries witch energy to send power into tools, it tunes them more closely to your aura. Here's a quick method for imbuing any tool with your Aries energy.

1. Place the tool in front of you on a table or altar.
2. Take a breath in, imagining that you are breathing in red-colored energy, and then say "Aries" as you exhale. Repeat this three times.
3. With a finger, trace the shape of your brows on your face. Then trace a line from the bridge of your nose to the tip. You've just traced the glyph for Aries.
4. Now, using the same finger, trace the glyph of Aries over or on the tool you are charging. Repeat this several times and imagine the glyph being absorbed by the tool.
5. Pick up the tool, take in a breath while imaging red energy, then blow that charged breath over the tool.

6. Say "Blessed be!" and proceed with using the tool or putting it away.

Hopefully this charging practice will inspire you and encourage you to experiment. Develop the habit of using the name *Aries* as a word of power, the glyph for Aries for summoning power, and the ruddy colors of Aries to visualize its flow. Feel free to use these spontaneously. Whether it be a pendulum, a wand, a crystal, a chalice, a ritual robe, or anything else that catches your imagination, these simple methods can have a large impact. The Aries energy you imprint into objects will be quick to rise and answer your call.

A Spell to Finish What You Start

By Jack Chanek

Aries are famous for our passion and indomitable wills. However, people born with the Sun in Aries sometimes struggle to follow through on our tasks. It is easy to get caught up in the excitement of something new and let old projects fall by the wayside, so that we fall into a cycle of starting things and never finishing them. This spell draws on the symbolism of the Two of Wands from the tarot deck, which is associated with Aries and represents will, planning, and goal setting. With the magical aid of the Two of Wands, you can tie yourself to a project and ensure that you stick with it long enough to complete it.

You will need:

+ The Two of Wands from your favorite tarot deck

+ Two wooden dowels, approximately 12" long

+ A 12" red ribbon made of cotton, silk, or another natural material

+ Dragon's Blood incense

+ A pen

59

Instructions:

Place the Two of Wands faceup in the center of your working space. Light the incense. Take a moment to meditate and find your center, then declare the purpose of the spell:

> *The will of the witch is the greatest tool of all.*
> *Today, I direct my will to [your goal].*
> *I declare that I shall see it done,*
> *and nothing shall sway me from my purpose.*
> *Bear witness, great powers of magic, for what I will, I do!*

Use the pen to write your goal on one side of the ribbon. Then, cross the dowels over each other. Wrap the ribbon around the dowels several times at the point where they cross, binding them together in an X shape. As you do so, repeat the following chant:

> *X marks the spot! The target's made and set.*
> *I draw my bow and loose my will; the arrow flies true.*
> *To get what can be got, I vow my strain and sweat.*
> *I shall not quit or quail until I've done what I must do.*

Tie a knot in the ribbon to secure it. Keep the chant going as you pass the X through the incense smoke, perfuming it thoroughly. When you have finished perfuming your talisman, place it in the center

60

of your working space, on top of the Two of Wands. Declare the completion of the spell:

So mote it be!

Place the talisman in your office, on your altar, or somewhere you will see it every day. Keep it there until you have finished what you set out to do. Then, ritually dispose of it by burning it in a fireplace or in another controlled fire. As you place it in the fire, say,

Great powers of magic, take heed!
The arrow has found its mark.
I have worked my will and finished my task,
and now I lay this charm to rest.

HERBAL
CORRESPONDENCES

These plant materials all have a special connection to your energy as an Aries witch. There are many more, but these are a good starting point.

Herbs	
Tobacco	offering to spirits, to help win a conflict, for focusing energy
Tarragon	for bravery, to dispel negative energy, to build confidence
Cayenne	to speed up spells, to create wards and boundaires, to releases attachments

Flowers

Red Geranium	warns of trouble, cleanses auras, brings good luck
Red Poppy	work with the dead, eases heart-ache, cools down overcharged auras
Honeysuckle	opens psychic gifts, promotes positivity, reduces anger

Incense and Fragrances

Frankincense	elevates consciousness, purifies spaces, improves concentration
Clove	helps find things, stimulates senses, dissipates illusions
Dragon's Blood	amplifies power, astral travel, draws fire energy

CLEANSING AND SHIELDING

Diotima Mantineia

An Aries witch meets life head-on. We enthusiastically engage with others in play, or partnership, or conflict. This leaves us open to getting tangled in toxic energy that comes our way either by accident or design. So, it's important for us to keep up with regular cleansing and protection work!

I learned this the hard way back in the nineties when I owned a small book/magical supply store and was very open about being a witch. This was during the time of the Satanic Panic, and most of us were in the closet with the door locked. Coven oaths of secrecy were taken very seriously because people's jobs and the custody of their children were at risk if word got out that they were a witch.

But I had no children and was my own boss, so I figured I could do my part to educate the public. And over the next few years, with Halloween write-ups in local papers, a stint as the Official Witch of an alternative radio station (I did short tarot readings on the air during rush hour for people who called in), and a few public rituals, my store and I became targets for a lot of negative energy from prayer groups and other people who were either fearful or jealous.

Fortunately, I had lots of books, excellent teachers, and a supportive magical community, so I learned quickly how to detect negative energy that came my way, and how to keep myself and my store clean and protected. Over the years I've continued to study and learn different ways of cleansing and shielding—magic always fascinates me. Here are some methods of cleansing and shielding I've found to be particularly useful and in tune with my Aries nature.

Cleansing

Let's start with cleansing. It's something we should do frequently, because it's hard to be out in the world and not pick up some squirrely energies.

An Aries' instinctive response to an attack is to counterattack. We aren't afraid of a fight, and attacks are fairly easy to discern, including magical/energetic ones. But actual magical attacks are relatively rare. It's the constant drip, drip, drip of negativity that sticks to us and little by little drags us down.

One time, a man came in my store on a rainy day, and instead of leaving his dripping umbrella by the door, he carried it with him as he browsed the shelves. I confronted him about it (as diplomatically as an irritated Aries can), and he was quite apologetic. He was simply unconscious of the fact that he was trailing water and endangering others who might slip on it.

I realized as I was mopping up after him that this was exactly what people often do on an energetic level. Soaked in toxic thoughts and emotions, they unconsciously leave a trail behind them wherever they go. Then equally unconscious, unguarded people may soak up the noxious miasma as they go by.

Weekly Cleansing Ritual

It's for this reason that I try to do a magical cleansing bath or shower at least once a week. Here's a simple method that won't take too much time.

First, make sure your bathroom is clean and orderly. Next, assemble the materials you will need in the kitchen.

You will need:

- + A half-gallon pitcher
- + A small saucepan
- + A handful of salt
- + Two or three of any of the following herbs (a small handful if dried, about twice that if fresh): rosemary, lemon balm, lavender, parsley, garden sage, lemon peel, hyssop (Hyssopus officinalis), anise hyssop (Agastache foeniculum)

Fill the pitcher with water. Hold your hands over the water (there are energy centers in your hands) and say,

Water is a blessing to all on Earth, and I am grateful.

I charge this water to my purpose
To cleanse me of all negative or inharmoni-
  ous energies
And carry them away to be transformed.

Pour about three cups of the water into the saucepan, and put it aside.

Take the salt and put it in the palm of your hand. Cover it with your other hand and say,

Salt of the Earth, I give thanks for the gift of
  your presence and blessings.
I call upon your cleansing powers to draw out
  and neutralize any negative or inharmo-
  nious energies that have attached them-
  selves to me.

Pour the salt into the water in the pitcher and stir it clockwise with your dominant hand until it is dissolved.

Put the saucepan on the stove and bring the water to a boil, then reduce it to a low simmer. One by one, take each of the herbs in the palm of your hand and say,

Spirit of [name of herb], *I give thanks for*
the gift of your presence and blessings.
I call upon your healing powers to cleanse me
of any negative or inharmonious energies
that have attached themselves to me.

Put the herbs in the simmering water, turn off
the stove, and let the herbs steep. As they are steeping, focus on your intention of cleansing yourself.
Stare at the steeping herbs and let your eyes imbue
the water with your intention. After about five or
ten minutes, strain out the herbs and pour the tea
into the pitcher.

Take a shower and clean yourself as you normally would. Then turn off the shower and slowly
pour the water from the pitcher over your head and
let it run down your body. Envision all negativity
being washed away. Alternatively, you can draw a
bath, pour the water into it, and soak in the bath,
making sure to dunk your head a few times.

Briefly rinse, dry yourself, and get dressed. It's
time to do some protection work!

Shielding

Another important tool for an Aries witch is a short daily protection spell. Aries are impatient. We want to get on with our day. So, short and effective is the way to go. I developed a little ritual for myself that I'll share below.

Before I get into the instructions, let me remind you of something you probably learned in high school biology class. Each of the cells in our bodies is surrounded by something called a semipermeable membrane. These membranes act kind of like a filter. They let in molecules that the cell needs while keeping other molecules out. It also works in the opposite direction—it keeps the cell together, and everything it needs inside, but it allows waste molecules to filter outside of the cell.

You'll want to visualize something similar around your entire body—a clear barrier that lets in the energies you need and want so you can stay connected to and aware of your environment, but blocks any harmful energies.

A Quick Shielding Ritual

This ritual involves gestures, words spoken aloud, and visualization (if you can't visualize, then focus in some other way on your intended results). Ideally, you will be able to do the whole routine, including the gestures and spoken words, on a daily basis, because that will set this spell into your subtle bodies so that when you need to be discrete, you can simply run through the spell in your mind, and it will still be effective. Here's what to do.

+ Stand facing east. Be aware of the four directions around you. Be aware of Earth beneath your feet, the stars above you.

+ Take a deep breath, sweeping your arms overhead, palms up (gathering fresh energy) as you inhale, then down in front of you, elbows bent, palms down (pushing out old, stale energy) as you exhale. Repeat two more times.

+ Bring your awareness fully into the present. Sense what you are seeing, hearing, feeling, smelling, and tasting. Notice your breath, and let it move into your belly.

Spend a few moments just paying attention to your breath, letting it reach a natural rhythm.

+ Envision the planet below your feet, with its fiery core. Sense a cord of red energy extending from the base of your spine to the planet's core. Know that you are supported by the planet itself, and you can draw energy from it, as well as releasing energies that need to be transformed into its central fire.

+ Envision the stars and infinite space above you. Sense a cord of white/silver energy reaching up from the crown of your head into space and connecting with the light from the stars, which imbue you with their light.

+ Visualize the cord of red Earth energy and the cord of white/silver star energy entwining together within your body, energizing and empowering you.

+ Now speak the following words, using the gestures indicated in brackets.

[Standing straight, feet slightly apart, arms by your sides.]

I am here, in this time, and this place.
The Earth is below me, the stars above me.

[Raise your arms out to your sides, shoulder height, palms up.]

Air, Fire, Water and Earth surround me.
[Visualize each of the elements in their direction as you speak them.]

I am rooted in the Earth.
[With arms still out, turn your palms down. Sense the energy centers in your palms connecting you to the Earth.]

I reach through the Stars.
[Palms turn up. Sense star energy coming into your palms.]

I come to my Center.
[Reach arms up overhead, bring palms together, then bring them to prayer position at your heart as you also bring your feet together. Now visualize

*the streams of light from Earth and sky entwining
along your spine and say the following:]*

**Within me, Earth and Sky entwine.
Blessed be.**
*[With palms still together, reach your hands up
over your head, then, with palms facing out, let
them arc down around you, visualizing an egg of
sparkling energy surrounding you. This energy
is protective, but not a block or a shield. It's your
very own semipermeable membrane that lets in
energy that harmonizes with your own, but keeps
out negativity.]*

Then go about your day, knowing you are grounded,
energized, and protected!

More experienced witches can easily invent their own spell using tools and techniques that are part of their tradition or practice. I recommend, though, that you incorporate gestures, words spoken aloud, and visualization. And remember that this routine should be a daily practice, as in actually performing it, not just thinking about performing it.

Cleansing and shielding is never a one and done thing. You'll want to keep up with daily and weekly practices.

The best way to cleanse and protect is to modulate our own personal vibration to emit an energy that will not allow any hostile, problematical, or simply inharmonious energies directed at us to pass, while remaining open to whatever we want to let in.

Eventually, awareness of the energies in our environment, cleansing, and setting boundaries become almost automatic, a part of who we are. The stronger we become in our craft, the deeper our connection with our spirit allies, the more we radiate the power that comes from personal integrity and a strong connection with spiritual reality. What we radiate does more to banish negative energy than what we build around us.

Personally, I'm not yet at the place where what I radiate is strong enough to banish all negativity—very few people are. Hence, I keep up with the basic spell work, knowing that the work I do to cleanse and protect allows me to build my inner strength, magical power, and connection with spirit. It's a crucial part of the work of a witch.

Be the Kind of Aries Badass You Want to See in the World

By Crow Walker

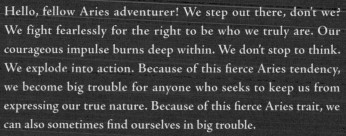

Hello, fellow Aries adventurer! We step out there, don't we? We fight fearlessly for the right to be who we truly are. Our courageous impulse burns deep within. We don't stop to think. We explode into action. Because of this fierce Aries tendency, we become big trouble for anyone who seeks to keep us from expressing our true nature. Because of this fierce Aries trait, we can also sometimes find ourselves in big trouble.

That's the cost for proverbially (or literally) stealing fire from the gods: bringing back not only the flame, but the lessons learned. As an Aries, I'm equally cool serving as an example of what to do—or what not to do. But either way, I want to shift the odds in my favor. The question is, how? I recommend using this grounding spell.

I know. The stillness of grounding seems like the Aries archnemesis. But what if it's not? There are as many methods for it as there are stars in the sky, from comingling our energy with the Earth's to letting go of the worries and frustrations of the day to become present in the moment. All these have their place, but this grounding spell speaks to the Aries heart. Because we're not only fighting for our right to express who we are in the world—we fight for everyone else to have that right, too. That is Aries magic.

You will need:

+ A mirror

Instructions:

Sit in a comfortable position, making sure you can see your reflection in the mirror. Soften your gaze as you look upon your reflection.

Breathe deeply, filling your lungs so your belly rises with each inhalation. With each breath, allow your gaze to soften further. Invite your heart to shine with the power of your Aries magic and speak the incantation below, the shining within you growing brighter with each word.

> *I call upon the bright Sun of my birth sign to shine its*
> *light upon the heart of my Aries magic: I AM.*
> *I call upon the bright Sun of my Aries magic to shine*
> *its light upon the threads of magic that connect me*
> *to others: WE ARE.*

Notice threads of light appear all around your reflection. They are the magical manifestation of your connections with your ancestors of blood and spirit, other living humans, river and tree, soil and stone. This is the web of life of which we are all a part. The web needs each of us and our unique expressions of who we are.

Feel this essential truth fuel the Aries power in your heart and ground you here and now. Say,

> *May my actions honor and serve my truth and*
> *the web of connection.*
> *May my Aries fire light the way for all.*
> *Blessed be.*

Now, go be the kind of Aries badass you want to see in the world!

WHAT SETS AN ARIES OFF, AND HOW TO RECOVER

Diotima Mantineia

It's not hard to aggravate an Aries. Mostly, it's just a brief thunderstorm—we don't stay upset at small things. But once we've decided something is "definitely a problem," you'll see the storm clouds gathering whenever that problem comes to our attention.

Different signs have different ways of reacting to events or words that cross an ethical or emotional boundary of theirs. Taureans might dig in their heels, or bellow loudly and start stomping around like the proverbial bull in a china shop. Cancers are likely to withdraw into their shells (protection mode) or scuttle away (avoidance mode). But an Aries' most common reaction to an important boundary of theirs being breached is to butt heads with who or whatever triggered them, then let everyone within shouting distance know just how angry they are. We tend to attack first and ask questions later.

I used to think anger was something that needed to be suppressed, until I realized suppressed anger doesn't go away. Inevitably, it surfaces in either an uncontrolled and damaging outburst, or it festers inside you. Either way, it ends up messing up your mental state, your relationships, and your physical health. We Aries need to find ways to manage and release anger, instead of suppressing it.

Identify the Triggers

The first step to using your anger instead of letting yourself get tripped up by it is to identify what triggers your anger and why. Recognize the anger when it comes up, and get clear on what exactly you are angry about. Sometimes the source of our anger is not obvious until we have given it some thought. Yeah, maybe you can't do it in the moment of rage, but when you've calmed down, take some time to identify what triggers you, and why.

While there are a lot of things that draw my Aries ire, carelessness and willful ignorance toward the health of the environment is a big one for me, particularly when it's perpetrated by those who profess to love nature and hold the Earth to be sacred. For instance, I dislike disposable electric candles. Their light is not the magical fire of a flame; it is encased in a polluting, nonrechargeable battery, surrounded by plastic. It's just more plastic junk that ends up in a landfill.

Their very existence aggravates me. But many of my friends use them, people I know do care about the environment and try to minimize their environmental impacts in other ways. I might say something to them about it, but I can't get angry with them, particularly when I know I'm guilty myself.

So, when I see electric candles, I take a deep breath, then direct my ire where it belongs—not at individuals, but at a society that is structured from the ground up to thoughtlessly consume nonrenewable resources and make it difficult for the average person to live in an environmentally sustainable way.

Unfortunately, getting angry at the entirety of modern civilization does nothing but flood my body with stress hormones. While I might redirect my anger to a different target, it's still messing with me. I'm still angry, and I need a way to release it.

Using Anger for Spells

Eventually, I learned to use my anger as a red flag. Once that flag pops up, I know I need to step back from my immediate emotional reaction, shift that energy, and direct it into a spell. That takes the energy away from me and puts it to good use.

The focus of the spell is changing the thing that angers you, righting the wrong. What you do, how you do it, will depend on your tradition and training. (If you are still a little light on training and spell work, a prayer to a deity or helping spirit is fine.) As you practice, you'll find it's possible to release your anger into the spell. And then your anger is no longer part of you. It's been burned like gasoline to power the engine of your spell.

Here's an example. My neighbor is an apple farmer on a very large scale. He harvests tens of thousands of bushels a year. Apple trees stretch across and down the mountain from my house to the road, and I know he has acreage elsewhere as well. He farms conventionally. To me, that is a problem. As an animist, I find modern farming methods to be highly problematic. But I am well-educated in agricultural realities, and I know there is nothing I can do or say that will convince him to change his ways. It would be difficult, expensive, and risky to switch his operation to organic methods. I can't blame him. He and his wife are good neighbors, nice people, and doing the best they can.

So, when I hear the tractor chugging through the trees, trailing the big cylinder that sprays huge arcs of pesticides from both sides, I take my anger at this to my deities, to the land spirits, and ask them to help me turn it into actions I can take that will help heal and strengthen the web of life here on my own land. And they do. Some of that action is practical, some of it is magical, but the action transforms my anger.

This is an important lesson I have learned about how to handle the anger that is so quick to surface from my Aries soul. I've discovered that, like most Aries, my anger is primarily sourced in a strong sense of justice, of what is right and what is wrong—at least in my eyes. Which led me to understand that anger is a helpful emotion if it is acknowledged and processed quickly. But if anger is held close, nurtured, and fed, it grows into something toxic.

I take the small actions I can, amplified by my magical intent and focus. Then, when I sit outside on an April night, watching the graceful arcs of spray illuminated in the lights of the Moon and the tractor, I can appreciate that beauty, and be fully present in the moment instead of stewing in righteous but impotent anger.

I bet you're wondering why he is spraying at night. It's because in April, the trees are in flower, and the bees he needs to pollinate his crop don't fly at night, so they won't get hit by the killing spray. Over the past few decades there's been an increasing awareness of nature's limits and the effect of our farming procedures on the broader ecosystem. I take comfort in this and in my conviction that we will change our ways—learn to live and farm in sustainable ways. Something I can contemplate in my now-peaceful state of mind.

This is not to say I won't speak up to individuals if I think it will do some good. Something else that gets on my last nerve (and it could be said that Aries only have one) is the use of Styrofoam, particularly at Pagan gatherings.

I have made myself unpopular at times by first asking fellow campers at a gathering whether the Earth and its web of life are a key part of their spiritual and/or magical practice. The answer was almost always an enthusiastic yes. Then I would point out that it would take only a little effort, and maybe a few more dollars, to at least purchase compostable tableware made with recycled materials, as opposed to using something that was made from one of the most toxic manufactured products on Earth, polluting the very planet so integral to their spiritual work.

So, yeah, that information was not always taken well. I've gotten a bit more tactful over the years, and I've learned to make sure I fully let go of any anger and irritation before speaking. I feel better for at least having taken action and given them information they may not have had, and some ideas to think about.

One of the actions I took not long after I moved to my land here in the mountains was to become a beekeeper. Bees are peaceful souls, spending their days collecting nectar, tending the baby bees, and making honey. But when they feel threatened, they react with something that seems very similar to what we call anger. Beekeepers try to avoid angering the bees not because they're afraid of getting stung (a good bee suit takes care of that), but because stinging anything kills a honeybee. The stinger stays in its target, ripping apart the body of the bee.

Anger can be fatal to humans, too. It's a powerful emotion that affects our bodies as well as our minds. It should be handled with care and respect. That means identifying and processing the anger before acting. Every sign has lessons to learn. Managing anger is one of ours.

We're wired to experience anger, irritation, antagonism—all those emotions that mean "no." We're a bit touchy and quick to react to perceived wrongs. When we say no, we're willing to back it up with action.

We're also wired for courage. An Aries will run, not walk, to where angels fear to tread. We want to make a difference, and we can. Aries are fighters at heart. And a skilled fighter learns quickly that strategy, thought, and planning are essential to an effective outcome.

When anger comes up for me, I've learned to let it point me toward a thoughtful, measured response that is directed appropriately, instead of an immediate, knee-jerk reaction. When I feel anger, I know something is wrong; something needs to be fixed. But instead of lashing out, mostly I find I can step back for a moment, identify the issues, plan my response. Then I let the anger drain away—it's done its job. I take action. I do what needs to be done. That's what Aries are best at.

A BRIEF BIO OF MARGOT ADLER

✳ ✳ ✳

Lilith Dorsey

Aries folks like myself are known for being first, fierce, and formidable. Margot Adler (1946–2014) was no exception. In many ways, she was the first voice of witchcraft a lot of us heard, either through her amazing work on WBAI, and later NPR, or in her groundbreaking book *Drawing Down the Moon*, first published in 1979. She went on to write more titles on topics ranging from revolution to vampires.

Aries are known for being innovative, intelligent, and edgy. In these respects, Margot delivered, just like New York City, the place she called home. I was proud to call Margot a friend. Featured as the High Priestess in the New York Tarot by Giani Siri, she was an icon of feminine power. She spoke about the divine feminine in a way that many had never heard, not in this lifetime anyway. Aries are by definition fire, and everything Margot Adler did was lit.

Some days, I'm afraid everyone will forget … forget what it was like to be around Margot Adler, and all my friends who have drifted across the veil. I know people will remember the books, the talks, the recorded information. But these people made history, and my heart is all too heavy.

One of the things I cherished about Margot Adler was that she knew her stuff. Paganism today is too often reconstituted drivel, and I say that as both an academic and a member of this community for over three decades. Fortunately, that wasn't who Margot Adler was; she delighted in discussing almost every topic, making sure you also knew what her cause célèbre was in the process.

Personally, it was a sublime privilege to have her at my rituals. If I think back, she was one of the first prominent people in the community to come out and support and dance and join us in honoring the New Orleans Voodoo pantheon. Margot Adler was a visionary, and the community will forever feel her loss. As her friend, I am sad we will not be able to smile and shake our stuff together in the same way again. I will continue to celebrate her memory and her spirit; I will try my best to know my stuff, and to always know where it came from, too. I'll remind people what a joyous and open spirit she had and dance a little more for her. I hope you will, too.

A Sampling of Aries Occultists

ORION FOXWOOD
faery seer and author
(April 11, 1962)

LINDA GOODMAN
astrologer and poet
(April 9, 1925)

RAVEN GRIMASSI
witch elder and author
(April 12, 1951)

NIGEL G. PEARSON
witch, herbalist, and author
(March 31, 1961)

GEORGE PICKINGILL
cunning man and witch
(April 2, 1816)

AMY ZERNER
tarotist, artist, and fashion designer
(March 23, 1951)

THE SWAY OF YOUR MOON SIGN

Ivo Dominguez, Jr.

The Moon is the reservoir of your emotions, thoughts, and all your experiences. The Moon guides your subconscious, your unconscious, and your instinctive response in the moment. The Moon serves as the author, narrator, and the musical score in the ongoing movie in your mind that summarizes and mythologizes your story. The Moon is like a scrying mirror, a sacred well, that gives answers to the question of the meaning of your life. The style and the perspective of your Moon sign shapes your story, a story that starts as a reflection of your Sun sign's impetus. The remembrance of your life events is a condensed subjective story, and it is your Moon sign that summarizes and categorizes the data stream of your life.

In witchcraft, the Moon is our connection and guide to the physical and energetic tides in nature, the astral plane, and other realities. The Moon in the heavens as it moves through signs and phases also pulls and pushes on your aura. The Moon in your birth chart reveals the intrinsic qualities and patterns in your aura, which affect the form your magick takes. Your Sun sign may be the source of your essence and power, but your Moon sign shows how you use that power in your magick. This chapter describes the twelve possible arrangements of Moon signs with an Aries Sun and what each combination yields.

♈

Moon in Aries

Having both your Sun and Moon in Aries is a call to be more self-aware and present in your life. Having the Moon in the same sign as your Sun means that it isn't really providing a second opinion to temper your thoughts and actions. This much drive and energy can lead you to great accomplishment or have you ricocheting through life and missing the mark.

It is hard for this combination to stay calm and still, and it is easy for emotions to boil over and sparks to fly. Having your Moon in Aries means that you need to stay centered. This double Aries combination also means you are driven to respond and react quickly. In some settings this is perfect, and in others it will lead to loss and troubles. Picking the right course requires making sure your gut instinct is balanced with thought. The time you take to think things through will save you time and trouble in the end.

You can be an unstoppable force of nature when you are pursuing your dreams and desires. Sometimes this means that you will bulldoze right through obstacles at the cost of relationships. You will be happier if you train yourself to be aware and responsive of other people's needs and perspectives. Aim for affirmation, but at the least achieve tolerance so you can cooperate and collaborate with others. The consideration and kindness you learn to offer others will also help you when you are at odds with yourself. Sun and Moon in Aries can be one of the most positive combinations when its power is handled with composure and wisdom.

An Aries Moon, like all the fire element Moons, easily stretches forth to connect with the energy of other beings. The fiery qualities cleanse and protect your aura from picking up other people's emotional debris or being influenced by your environment. It is relatively easy for you to blend your energy with others and to separate cleanly. However, you must be careful to not use up too much energy or burn yourself out. Learning to sense your flow and to moderate it is essential. The energy field and magic of an Aries Moon tend to move and change faster than any other sign, but it is harder to hold to a specific task or shape. This can be overcome with self-awareness and practice.

Moon in Taurus

This earthy Moon does not put out that Aries fire; rather, it gives it a proper container. A Taurus Moon gives you more tenacity, persistence, and follow-through in your actions. This Taurus Moon helps you be more considerate and diplomatic, lessening the brashness that many attribute to Aries. This

Moon makes you more generous and giving of your time to others. It makes it easier to work with people and act as a leader. You are still an Aries Sun and prone to following your own counsel above anything else, but if you listen to your Moon, you'll go farther. On those rare occasions when you find yourself overthinking things, tune in to the down-to-Earth instinct of a Taurus Moon to get unstuck.

This Moon also helps slow you down enough so that you can think a bit before leaping into action. This Moon encourages you to stop and smell the roses, to enjoy the world around you. Your quality of life as an Aries is better when counterbalanced by Taurean sensuality. In astrology, the Moon is said to be exalted in Taurus, which means it favors success and good fortune. For an Aries, this means added charm to get your way, and if that doesn't work, then the endurance for a long struggle. The Taurean influence also provides more ease in understanding the properties of material things, whether this be in the practical matters of business or the best use of a medium in the arts.

A Taurus Moon, like all the earth element Moons, generates an aura that is magnetic and pulls energy inward. This Moon also makes it easier to create strong shields and wards. If something does manage to breach your shields or create some other type of energetic injury, get some healing help, or the recovery may take longer than it should. The auras of people with a Taurus Moon are excellent at holding or restoring a pattern or acting as a container or vessel in a working. Generally, people with a Taurus Moon have less flexibility in their aura. You can work toward improving your flexibility, but the quick fix is to create new boundaries or a larger container. Astral travel and other forms of soul travel are harder to begin with this Moon sign. However, once in motion, a stronger and more solid version of you travels than is true for most witches.

♊
Moon in Gemini

The most notable effect of a Gemini Moon is that the Aries energy bursts forth as a stream of communication. You text, you call, you hang out on social media, you find ways to collect and share information and opinions. Sometimes the enthusiasm of

Aries flowing through a Gemini Moon can be too much, and you offend, antagonize, or embarrass others or yourself. Used with care and skill, this is a great Sun and Moon combination for communication and persuasion. You can also tell stories and jokes in a way that lightens all troubles and fosters daring and adventurous undertakings. There is a tendency for hyperactivity that comes with this combination. When blocked, this hectic energy is often transmuted into anxiety. Under these circumstances, it becomes hard to hear constructive criticism, and it can become a negative feedback loop. Reel it all in and strike a path forward to break the loop.

You are a chameleon, a shape-shifter, and you can make yourself fit in or stand out by changing your mind and your words in an instant. This is not false, fickle, or inauthentic when you use this gift for the common good and to nudge the world in a forward-thinking direction. Aries likes to go forward at full speed, but a Gemini Moon makes you nimble so that you can swerve and change course. The key to making this Sun-Moon combination work is to form the habit of reminding yourself of your goals so you can get back on track. Ask yourself why you are doing what you are doing and if it leads somewhere useful.

A Gemini Moon, like all the air Moons, makes it easier to engage in soul travel and psychism and gives the aura greater flexibility. You are a quicksilver fire that seeks connection, but not a merger with other beings and energies. When an air type aura reaches out and touches something, it can quickly read and copy the patterns it finds. A Gemini Moon gives the capacity to quickly adapt and respond to changing energy conditions in working magick or using the psychic senses. However, turbulent spiritual atmospheres are felt strongly and can be uncomfortable or cause harm. A wind can pick up and carry dust and debris, and the same is true for an aura. If you need to cleanse your energy, become still, and the debris will simply fall out of your aura.

Moon in Cancer

This Moon encourages your Aries energy to focus on your emotions and matters of the heart. You are more emotional and sensitive than most other Aries and may have the gift of empathy or mediumship. This combination leans toward introversion and an active inner life. You may not appear as bold as some Aries, so you may be unrecognized for the powerhouse that you are. Think of this as useful camouflage and remember that your Sun and Moon are in cardinal signs. You can use your drive and intuition to navigate complicated situations while staying true to yourself. This process can be messy, and the sooner you become comfortable with laughing at your own foibles, the smoother your life will be.

The Aries affinity for being a warrior is steered by the Cancer Moon toward protecting others and taking on causes. Cancer Moon makes you more strongly devoted to the ideals of friendships, family of choice, and family of blood. Be sure that the people and causes you choose to champion explicitly want your help and the specific way you are giving assistance. You are mortified if you inadvertently hurt people, but your unbridled enthusiasm may worsen the harm unless reined in. There are many ways to prove yourself and follow your sense of duty without losing yourself in the process. Being a pioneer, a way finder, a scout on the cutting edge of spiritual and social matters is also satisfying to this Sun and Moon combination. The Moon is Cancer's ruling planet, so it has more power here. This placement combined with Aries can also give great creativity and charisma.

A Cancer Moon, like all the water Moons, gives the aura a magnetic pull that wants to merge with whatever is nearby. Imagine two drops of water growing closer until they barely touch and how they pull together to become one larger drop. The aura of a person with a Cancer Moon is more likely to retain the patterns and energies it touches. This can be a good thing or a problem depending on what is absorbed. You must take extra care to cleanse and purify yourself before and after magickal work whenever possible. One of the gifts that comes with this Moon is a capacity for healing touch that offers comfort while filling in, and healing disruptions in other people's energy.

Moon in Leo

Double the fire, but in this case, you have the cardinal and the fixed modalities of fire. It is almost like having a full Moon built into your chart. You love to shine and do so with ease. Your heart draws you to adventure, and you have a romantic and idealistic outlook on life. Depending on other factors in your chart, this may be either an inward pursuit or one that the whole world sees. There is a dance in your heart that sways between the twin flames of achievement for your sake and for the sake of being seen. View this as having two sources of motivation rather than interpret it as problematic. Facing this truth will help you maintain your balance. There is nothing wrong with being fully yourself and occupying the space that is yours. The goal is to aspire to be a model of excellence that encourages others to step up rather than being the center of attention. Enjoy the praise and honors you receive, but do not become dependent on them for motivation.

Your knowledge of who you are and all your many skills does not immediately translate into real-world results. That Leo Moon charm and Aries Sun passion require planning, guidance, and follow-through to achieve real results. Additionally, your internal spotlight on what you can do makes it harder to see what parts of you need improvement and refinement. Soul-searching and a close examination of your life are acts of will for you, not instinctive or automatic behaviors. The arts in any form, really all creative endeavors, are good for personal evolution and self-care.

A Leo Moon, like all the fire element Moons, easily stretches forth to connect with the energy of other beings, though a little bit less than Aries and Sagittarius. The fiery qualities cleanse and protect your aura from picking up other people's emotional debris or being influenced by your environment. It is relatively easy for you to blend your energy with others and to separate cleanly. The Leo Moon also makes it easier for you to find your center and stay centered. The fixed fire of Leo makes it easier to hold large amounts of energy that can be applied for individual and collective workings. You are particularly well suited to ritual leadership or the role of being the primary shaper of energy in a working.

Moon in Virgo

This is a challenging or potentially inspiring Moon for an Aries to have. The Virgo Moon loves getting the details right and perfect planning. The Aries Sun wants to jump straight in and fly by the seat of their pants. However, if these two styles can be brought into harmony, this produces a sharp discerning mind backed by a strong will. You want the best from yourself and from other people. Once again, balance is very important if you wish to live your best life. Formal training and structured learning, whether in academic matters, business, or witchcraft, will serve you well. In addition to gaining knowledge and skills, an organized approach will reduce your stress level. You also have a wide range of interests, and the only way you'll manage to do half the things on your list is with careful planning.

You have an inclination toward evaluating, scoring, and judging everything. This includes you, the people in your life, and the world in general. Your desire to aim for your personal best helps you polish the jewel of your soul. It becomes a problem when this discernment turns into harsh judgment that stifles the motivation to do better. This can affect you, and it can affect all your relationships, family, friends, and coworkers. Train yourself to listen to what you say and envision the impact it has. Ask yourself whether the results are productive or destructive. It is important to make it a habit to give yourself and others praise for making a good effort or correcting mistakes.

A Virgo Moon, like all the earth element Moons, generates an aura that is magnetic and pulls energy inward. This Moon also makes it easier to create strong thoughtforms and energy constructs. You have strong shields, but if breached, your shields will tend to hang on to the pattern of injury; get some healing help or the recovery may take longer than it should. Virgo Moons are best at perceiving and understanding patterns and processes in auras, energy, spells, and so on. You can be quite good at spotting what is off and finding a way to remedy the situation. This gives the potential to do healing work and curse breaking, among other things. This Moon's mutable earth combined with the cardinal fire of Aries can give you insights into the mysteries of plants and animals.

♎
Moon in Libra

This is not an easy combination to manage, so it is a good thing that Aries can be very determined. Normally an Aries is sure of what they want, and they follow their passion wherever it might lead them. Libra Moon tends to make the needs and emotions of other people important to you. Conflict and peace are both part of you and your work. It is productive to view the world as a diplomat or a mediator who strives for fairness and practicality. Don't confuse thinking through every angle and possibility as being the same as taking action. It may feel as if you have because you will have engaged in a considerable effort. It is only when you have made a distinct choice and followed through on that choice that your Aries nature will be satisfied.

This Moon also imparts aesthetic sensibilities, a creative flair, and an aptitude for creating beauty. This can express itself in arts, creative endeavors, and day-to-day life. It can also be mostly internalized as flights of imagination and daydreaming. This can be delightful, but unless you reach goals so you can set off to pursue a new one, you feel less satisfied over time. Remind yourself that the wind from this air sign Moon is meant to fan your flame, not put it out. Libra Moon also makes you think of love, friendships, and all relationships in an idealized way. Be careful that you do not put people on pedestals, or at the least not tall ones. This makes it confusing or painful when you are met with coldness, or your needs are disregarded. Don't overthink it; be direct and clear the air. Live on your own terms and keep the people who know and respect you.

A Libra Moon, like all the air Moons, makes it easier to engage in soul travel and psychism and gives the aura greater flexibility. When you are working well with your Libra Moon, you can make yourself a neutral and clear channel for information from spirits and other entities. You are also able to tune in to unspoken requests when doing divinatory work. The auras of people with Libra Moon are very capable at bridging and equalizing differences between the subtle bodies of groups of people. This allows you to bring order and harmony to energies raised and shaped in a group ritual.

♏

Moon in Scorpio

The action never stops when an Aries has a Scorpio Moon. You have vitality, desires, intensity, confidence, and a personality made of many swirling layers of passion and emotion. You give the impression of strength and competence even when you are pushing through real adversity and imagined problems. You are very persuasive and can convince people to follow your ideas. If people aren't on board with your plan, then you do it yourself. You try to bend the shape of the world to suit you, and to some degree, you succeed. This is likely to be a repeating pattern, so strive to make it one that leads to a better and happier life.

This means that it is doubly important for you to do deep soul-searching. Your innate skepticism and distrust of authority can serve you well to find deep truths. However, if your seeking and research is too influenced by suspicion and a defensive outlook, you will see connections, conspiracies, and dangers where there are none.

Scorpio is water of the fixed modality, water under pressure, which makes your emotions more extreme. This gives you a powerful sexual nature, a great yearning to connect with others and to guard against that connection, and deep wells of creative and destructive impulses. To those whom you give your trust, you are generous, caring, and protective. When you gain control, or at least an understanding, of the turbulence you carry within you, most of your goals will be attainable. Perhaps more importantly, you'll have a sense of clarity and personal meaning that renews your relationship with life. Your strong psychic skills will serve you much better when you can sort through your impressions with a more detached perspective.

A Scorpio Moon, like all the water Moons, gives the aura a magnetic pull that wants to merge with whatever is nearby. You easily absorb information about other people, spirits, places, and so on. If you are not careful, the information and the emotions will loop and repeat in your mind. To release what you have picked up, acknowledge what you perceive and then reframe its meaning in your own words. The energy and magick of a Scorpio Moon are adept at probing and moving past barriers, shields, and wards. This also gives you the power to remove things that should not be present.

Moon in Sagittarius

Double fire produces a love of freedom, independence, and honor. Truth in all caps and bold print is one of the central deities in your personal pantheon. You do best when you feel your activities are connected to a larger purpose or a cause. In the times that your focus is at its strongest, your mental faculties blaze with passion and your emotions are cool and dispassionate. There is risk of coming across as arrogant unless you explain the reasons for your words and actions. Your code of ethics is important to you, but it is hard for others to figure it out because you are so flexible and like to test limits. This Moon encourages you to speak directly, bluntly at times, so it is vital that you pay attention to the impact you have on others. Although you enjoy winning, you also want to be seen and understood, which requires fully reciprocal communication.

When your Moon sign is Sagittarius, especially combined with an Aries Sun, you have a strong wanderlust, a restlessness, a wide-ranging curiosity that draws you to different cultures, places, spiritualities, and so on. You have a gift for getting other people excited and motivated to explore the world and expand their minds. If you can travel, you will, and if you can't, then you'll explore via books and the internet. You love the big picture, big theories, and big principles, and you understand them. The real work for you is in convincing yourself to pause to take in the details because they are important. If you need a mental trick to help you pay attention to the details, remind yourself that there are worlds within worlds.

When you look at the small things, broad new vistas will reveal themselves.

The auras of people with Sagittarius Moon are the most adaptable of the fire Moons. Your energy can reach far and change its shape easily. You are particularly good at affecting other people's energy or the energy of a place. Like the other fire Moons, your aura is good at cleansing itself, but it is not automatic and requires your conscious choice. This is because the mutable fire of Sagittarius is changeable and can go from a small ember to a pillar of fire that reaches the sky. It is important that you manage your energy so it is somewhere between the extremes of almost out and furious inferno.

♑

Moon in Capricorn

You have both the ram and the goat, which gives you all the muscle needed to batter, climb, and conquer what you choose to. No matter what soft or polished exterior you put on, underneath you are rock solid and unmovable in your convictions. You often know what needs to be said and done in almost any situation. Your sense of accomplishments comes from your deeds and not what others have to say. There are only a handful of people whose opinion truly matters to you. A Capricorn Moon makes it harder for you to be anything other than the boss. When you can't be in charge, be practical and apply your powers of persuasion to steer things in the direction you want. Don't waste energy on removing people who are obstacles; sidestep them or change their minds.

You want status, though you have mixed feelings about that desire. You don't need to be in the limelight or to have hordes of people around you; you just need to have a small solid group you trust. You are better off when the people closest to you also have goals and pursuits. You learn from watching them and are happier when you help them. Make seeking out your people, your family of choice, a priority, as they will help you become free of the limits of your past. If you don't do this, you may develop a harsh perspective on humanity's failings. You are not fated to be alone or lonely, though fixating on those worries may bring them about. It is crucial that you find and maintain a balance between your work and your personal life. It is easy for you to become obsessive about your projects. If you find yourself being possessive or controlling or becoming the target of those feelings or behaviors, attend to it immediately.

A Capricorn Moon, like all the earth element Moons, generates an aura that is magnetic and pulls energy inward. What you draw to yourself tends to stick and solidify, so be wary, especially when doing healing work or cleansings. The magick of a Capricorn Moon is excellent at imposing a pattern or creating a container in a working. Your spells and workings tend to be durable. You also have a knack for building wards and doing protective magick. With proper training, you are good at manifesting the things you need.

♒ Moon in Aquarius

You do love being unpredictable and you love being surprised, even though you are good at predicting trends. You live life at a faster rate than is comfortable for many. You thrive on new experiences and like to dive in and get fully involved in whatever catches your interest. The search for the meaning of life will always be on your mind. Despite your desire to be in the thick of things, you are also cautious about getting too close to people. Your rebellious nature and preference to ignore rules, boundaries, and attachments are so important to you that you may unintentionally hurt others. You care about humanity as a concept but have a hard time dealing with the imperfections of individuals. Try to give people more time and space; you process things at a faster rate than most. You enjoy thinking about the future, and you wish it would arrive faster.

Taking risks to reap rewards comes as easily to you as breathing. However, you need to focus more on facts and observations than on following your gut. You have an aptitude for making the best use of the resources you have available and luck when it comes to finding more opportunities. You can be very charming and easily standout in any business or social setting. Your success comes from your understanding of the forces that shape the culture. This is what you need to keep in mind so that you are more patient and listen more deeply to people. Making compromises is not in your constitution, but they will speed you toward your goals. You are loyal to the people you've chosen to be in your inner circle. This is not always apparent to them, so take the time to show them what they mean to you.

Like all the air Moons, the Aquarius Moon encourages a highly mobile and flexible aura. Without a strong focus, the power of an air subtle body becomes scattered and diffuse. If you have an air Moon, an emphasis should be placed on finding and focusing on your center of energy. Grounding is important, but focusing on your core and center is more important. From that center, you can strengthen and stabilize your power. People with Aquarius Moon are good at shaping and holding a specific thoughtform or energy pattern and transferring it to other people or into objects.

Moon in Pisces

Pisces is the last sign and Aries is the first, and in you, the beginning and the end meet. In a sense, you are betwixt and between, and your soul stands in two places at once. Pisces Moon brings out a great interest in spirituality and a sensitive soul. It is challenging to be an Aries who is aware of the overlapping waves of emotions and thoughts from all that surrounds them. This is a great gift when managed well, and when it is not, there can be apprehension and uneasiness. A central part of the work of being an Aries is self-development. With this Moon, it is imperative that you develop confidence and a deep belief in your ability to grow. Making sure that you have enough solitude will help you become clearer on what is yours and what you have absorbed from others. Others tend to see you as stronger and bolder than you feel inside.

You have deep wellsprings of creativity that merit expression and exploration. You are inventive and full of inspiration that can be applied in the arts, the sciences, or in business. The fiery Aries pressure to do more pushes on the mutable waters of Pisces, and it is best to keep things flowing. If you don't have enough opportunity for self-expression or block the flow, it can turn into fretting and brooding. Your physical health also relies on keeping yourself unblocked. You would like the world to be more honorable and straightforward than it is. You have quite a bit going on, and when you get distracted and miss important dates, you'll be hard on yourself. Avoid this problem by making it your custom to take notes, enter reminders in your calendar, and do anything else that will structure your life.

With a Pisces Moon, the emphasis should be on learning to feel and control the rhythm of your energetic motion in your aura. Water Moon sign auras are flexible, cohesive, and magnetic, so they tend to ripple and rock like the action of waves. Pisces Moon is the most likely to pick and hang on to unwanted emotions or energies. Rippling your energy and bouncing things off the outer layers of your aura is a good defense. Be careful, develop good shielding practices, and make cleansing yourself and your home a regular practice. The energy of people with Pisces Moon is best at energizing, comforting, and healing disruptions in other people's auras.

TAROT
CORRESPONDENCES

♈

You can use the tarot cards in your work as an Aries witch for more than divination. They can be used as focal points in meditations and trance to connect with the power of your sign or element or to understand them more fully. They are great on your altar as an anchor for the powers you are calling. You can use the Minor Arcana cards to tap into Mars, Sun, or Venus in Aries energy, even when they are in other signs in the heavens. If you take a picture of a card, shrink the image and print it out; you can fold it up and place it in spell bags or jars as an ingredient.

Aries Major Arcana

The Emperor

All the Fire Signs

The Ace of Wands

Aries Minor Arcana

2 of Wands	Mars in Aries
3 of Wands	Sun in Aries
4 of Wands	Venus in Aries

• MY MOST ARIES WITCH MOMENT •

Diotima Mantineia

my most Aries witch moments—good, funny, and not-so-great—have all included fire. Fire is Aries' element, and my Sun is not the only planet I have in the sign. Mercury and Jupiter are there as well, and with Pluto in Leo (another fire sign), the element is strong in my natal chart.

I always loved campfires as a kid, but it wasn't until I went to my first Pagan gathering and danced around a huge bonfire intentionally set for trance dancing at the center of a drum circle that I truly understood the magic and power of the element.

The campground—two hundred acres in the woods of northwest Maryland, on the banks of the magnificent Susquehanna River—was a magical place, and the gathering itself was a whole new experience for me. At the time, I had only been identifying as a witch for a few years, and most of my interactions with other witches were limited to the two covens I had studied with and a few low-key local gatherings.

This was pre-internet and at the height of the Satanic Panic, so finding other witches was far more difficult, as most of us were hiding deep in the proverbial broom closet. But at the gathering, I found myself surrounded by several hundred other witches and Pagans being as witchy and Paganish and as far out of the closet as they wanted to be in this safe space. Flags and banners with esoteric symbols flew over campsites, small altars sprouted in front of them, craftspeople displayed their magical wares in booths, and the scents of different incenses were always in the air. It was colorful and magical, and I was entranced. Plus, I got to camp out on this beautiful land where the land spirits were strong and (mostly) benign.

Some friends and I followed the drums down to the fire the first night. I sat and watched for a while, but I love to dance, and eventually I joined the dancers circling the fire. No stranger to trance, I found the heat and the flames and the drums took me into a different kind of trance than I'd experienced before. Like most trance experiences, it's difficult to put into words, but suffice it to say that I connected deeply with the land, particularly the nearby Susquehanna and the still, small pond only a few yards away from the bonfire. It was a profound experience that opened new paths for me.

Since then, I've danced around many other fires. Some were more conducive to trance experiences than others. So much depends on the community. I learned the important role firekeepers play in building and maintaining the fire, approaching it as a spiritual/magical task with clear intentions. The vibes are very different at a fire with designated, experienced firekeepers, rather than just a few people occasionally throwing more wood on a carelessly constructed fire.

Eventually, I learned to drum, which gave me a different and equally valuable perspective on the fire, the dancers, and the drums. I could watch instead of feeling the flow of energy between the dancers and the fire and synchronize with the drums. But I still prefer to dance—one reason being that it gets me closer to the fire.

As much as I love working with fire, it's important to never forget that it is volatile, dangerous, and can shift from a quiet flame to a blaze in just a few moments, especially if the candle or fire has been magically charged. I learned that lesson the time I nearly burned my house down.

I had attended a public ritual put on by a local organization I have ties to. As part of the ritual, everyone got a tea light, which they charged, put on the altar, and lit. It made for a lovely altar, but there hadn't been enough time to let the tea lights burn all the way down before everyone left, and discarding them half burned was not a good option. So, I took them home with me, figuring I'd just put them on a metal tray and let them burn down on my stovetop, which seemed like a safe place.

This would have been fine if they'd all stayed put in their little metal cups. But I had apparently not set them far enough apart. For a while, they were burning quietly, then suddenly they became a single sheet of flame over a foot high. I grabbed a fire extinguisher and put it out before any real damage was done, but it was a scary moment, and a major cleanup job on both the physical and magical levels.

The incident inspired a few long talks with myself and some helpful spirits about how I had been handling energy. I've always held that almost every magical working brings results if you pay attention. Even the ones that fall flat, or boomerang on you, will offer some kind of a clue as to why they didn't work out as intended. This one certainly did!

There was another, much more fun, incident where the fire went out of bounds. It was Halloween/Samhain night, and I went over to a friend's house. She lived in a great neighborhood for trick-or-treating and decorated her house accordingly. We had decided to play witches for the kids who came to the door, then, after the costumed hordes had returned to their homes, to do a brief Samhain ritual. It was a lovely night out, and we briefly considered doing the ritual on the deck, but eventually we decided to do it in her dining room, where she had already set up an altar.

She had recently bought an oil lamp in the shape of a skull from a local ceramic artist and given it pride of place on the altar for its initiatory lighting. As I was calling fire, facing south, back to the altar, she interrupted me to say, "We're taking this outside." I was shocked at the interruption. "At least wait until I've finished the call!" She replied, "NOW, Diotima!" I turned around to see her carrying the skull at arm's length, flames shooting from its eyes, out the door to the deck.

Once the skull was safely ensconced on the picnic table on the deck, we started laughing hysterically, and we ended up finishing the ritual out on the deck. Maybe that's where we were supposed to be in the first place.

That incident was a good reminder that Samhain does not have to be Very Serious. The ancestors and spirits like a good laugh, too. I know they were laughing along with us that night!

Because I love fire so much, I use it a lot in my personal magic. There is one excellent technique I want to share with you because it is perfectly suited to the Aries witch.

Epsom Salts Fire

This is as close as you can come to having a (safe!) bonfire on your altar. You can use it to clear the space, which it does very well, but you can also use it to make an offering, burn petition papers, or perform a divination.

You will need:

- A fireproof container and lid and a plate to put it on. I like to use a small cast-iron cauldron. Some people use a sturdy ceramic mug or bowl. The lid should be large enough to quickly and completely cover the container if the fire needs to be smothered.
- Epsom salts
- 91% isopropyl (rubbing) alcohol, or a 151-proof liquor. I like alcohol for cleansing, liquor for offerings and petitions.
- Essential oils (optional)
- A long lighter or fireplace matches

Instructions:

The how-to of this is pretty easy, but the assembly should involve charging all the ingredients as you put them in the cauldron and speak your intention for the cleansing/offering/petition/divination.

Put the plate and dish somewhere isolated from anything flammable. The fire is unlikely to flare up, but it's still fire, which is unpredictable. Put the lid where you can easily grab it if you want to extinguish the fire.

You'll judge how much salt and alcohol to use by the size of the container you're using, but start small, until you get a feel for it. The proportions are two parts salt to one part alcohol. So, start with two tablespoons of salt and one tablespoon of alcohol.

You can add a drop or two of essential oils to the salt before adding the alcohol, but don't overdo it.

Put the salt in the container and pour the alcohol over it. Then touch the lighter or match to the salt, and you have fire!

When the fire has burned down, you will

need to let the container cool, then soak it at least overnight to get the salt out. You may need to chip at it with a dull knife, so keep that in mind when choosing your container. Depending on what you used the fire for, you can dispose of the salt by letting it flow down the drain, tossing it in a stream or river, or burying it.

I think you'll find this technique fun and useful for creating some perfect witchy moments for an Aries.

• YOUR RISING SIGN'S INFLUENCE •

Ivo Dominguez, Jr.

The rising sign, also known as the ascendant, is the sign that was rising on the eastern horizon at the time and place of your birth. In the birth chart, it is on the left side on the horizontal line that divides the upper and lower halves of the chart. It is often said that the rising sign is the mask that you wear to the world, but it is much more than that. It is also the portal through which you experience the world. The sign of your ascendant colors and filters those experiences. Additionally, when people first meet you, they meet your rising sign. This means they interact with you based on their perception of that sign rather than your Sun sign. This in turn has an impact on you and how you view yourself. As they get to know you over time, they'll meet you as your Sun sign. Your ascendant is like the colorful clouds that hide the Sun at dawn, and as the Sun continues to rise, it is revealed.

The rising sign has an influence on your physical appearance as well as your style of dress. To some degree, your voice, mannerisms, facial expressions, stance, and gait are also swayed by the sign of your ascendant. The building blocks of your public persona come from your rising sign. How you arrange those building blocks is guided by your Sun sign, but your Sun sign must work with what it has been given. For witches, the rising sign shows some of the qualities and foundations for the magickal personality you can construct. The magickal personality is much more than simply shifting into the right headspace, collecting ritual gear, lighting candles, and so on. The magickal persona is a construct that is developed through your magickal and spiritual practices to serve as an interface between different parts of the self. The magickal persona, also known as the magickal personality, can also act as a container or boundary so that the mundane and the magickal parts of a person's life can each have its own space. Your rising also gives clues about which magickal techniques will come naturally to you.

This chapter describes the twelve possible arrangements of rising signs with an Aries Sun and what each combination produces. There are 144 possible basic kinds of Aries when you take into consideration the Moon signs and rising signs. You may wish to reread the chapter on your Moon sign after reading about your rising sign so you can better understand these influences when they are merged.

Aries Rising

With both your Sun and rising in Aries, there is no mistaking that you look and act like an Aries. This combination makes you more spontaneous and even more likely to rush headlong into things than an average Aries. You take stock of situations quickly, make choices, and get down to work. You find it easy to take on the role of a warrior or protector. Others see this in you and expect you to be their knight or their ranger. You do have a noble nature and are likely to feel called to do this kind of work. It is important that you mind your temper as this double dose of fire can lead to explosions. All your passions and appetites are quick to rise and often visible to other people. It's a good idea to be mindful of when you would be served better by throttling back and toning yourself down.

You like to be the best at everything, and you like to get there first. Be alert, or you may bulldoze over people or wreck situations you had carefully built. This much Aries energy intensifies your ambitions, which, when well controlled, is a great blessing. However, when your ambitions overrule your better nature, you can be unthinking and have the potential to misuse your power. There is a good chance of accumulating a growing list of enemies unless you learn to be more aware of your impact on the people around you.

An Aries rising means that when you reach out to draw in power, fire will answer first. If you need other types of energy, you need to reach further, focus harder, and be more specific in your request. This combination makes it easier for you to access pure life force for healing or magick. After doing magick or energy work, make sure you cool off and close down your connections to the power.

Taurus Rising

The solid earthiness of Taurus as your rising sign presents a front that is very different than who you are at your fiery core. Sometimes this is useful because it gives you more gravitas when you need to be taken seriously by others. This combination helps give your willpower a steadier foundation to work from. You appear more laid back than you are, so count on surprising people when you go from zero to warp speed. You have a greater need for security and stability than most Aries, especially in matters related to home and finances. In addition to the passionate nature of your Sun sign, you have a great degree of sensuality and a love of creature comforts.

Taurus is known for determination and stubbornness. Aries is known for knowing what they want and how they want to get it. Once you've made up your mind, it is hard to change it or the direction you've chosen. One of the advantages to a Taurus rising is that it slows down that impetuous Aries nature. This results in better-reasoned choices. This makes you more effective in a leadership situation.

Your physical health is better when you structure your eating and physical activities. You will be more comfortable in your body if you do so and will live a longer life.

Taurus rising gives more strength in your aura and the capacity to maintain a more solid shape to your energy. This gives you stronger shields and allows you to create thoughtforms and spells that are longer lasting. This combination also makes you a better channel for other people's energy in group work because you can tolerate larger volumes of different types of energies. After any kind of working, make sure your aura and energy return to your normal, because the Taurus rising likes to retain patterns.

♊

Gemini Rising

Fire and air are a powerful combination. The speed and drive of Aries are channeled into the mind and powers of communication of Gemini. Talking, writing, reading, plugging into social media, and keeping up with current affairs are part of who you are on a daily basis. Your aura buzzes with energy and a sense of activity even when you are perfectly still. When you are in action, you can zoom about, leaving a blur in your wake. You have a childlike, inquisitive attitude that keeps you young at heart and in touch with the world. Your curiosity can sometimes come across as a bit rude when you ask indelicate questions. There is also a predisposition to shift your attention quickly from topic to topic, person to person, and so on in a way that can be interpreted as being fickle or flighty. You are neither of those things, but your actions are easy to misunderstand. If that happens, turn on your ample charm and wit and explain what you think and feel. Please be heedful that though you have an abundance of interests and energy, you can still get overwhelmed by putting too many things on your to-do list. It won't do much good to ask you to cut things out of your list, so instead I'll suggest that you put reminders in your calendar to circle back to unfinished business.

Gemini rising enables powers of spiritual communication. It helps your energy and aura stretch farther and adapt to whatever it touches. You would do well to develop your receptive psychic skills as well as practices such as mediumship and channeling. This combination can also lend itself to communication with animals and plants. When you are worked up, you have a tendency to broadcast your thoughts and feelings to others. Sharpen up your shielding skills for the sake of privacy and peace.

Cancer Rising

This combination is complicated because your Aries Sun wants to rush forward and your Cancer rising wants to hang back. You oscillate between the contrasting characteristics of these two signs. Aries wants to answer a call to arms and Cancer wants to have a nurturing chat and some tea. You want to roam the world and stay cozy at home. This dynamic can cause strain and stress, but it can also be turned to your benefit. You have greater awareness of other people's emotions than most Aries. This can lead to better friendships and stronger relationships. The Cancer rising makes you a bit more cautious, which helps to counterbalance your risk-taking behavior. This ascendant urges you to look ahead before leaping.

The fire of your Aries Sun heats up the waters of your Cancer rising so your emotions are stormier. Your imagination is also powerful, quick, and changeable. Whether this is experienced as a plus or a minus is determined by how well you develop your will and emotional control. In the end, this means more passion and more emotion that can lift you to great heights or lay you low. Passion and emotion are energy that can push you around or can be directed to the goals you desire.

Cancer rising grants the power to use your emotions, or the emotional energy of others, to power your witchcraft. Though you can draw on a wide range of energies to fuel your magick, raising power through emotion is the simplest. Your Aries fire passing through the influence of Cancer gives you energy that is useful for doing emotional healing and calming others. When there is a strong need, you have an aura of influence that is very persuasive. You can also extend your shield to protect others.

Leo Rising

Everything about you is a bit bigger than life, pops, and sparkles. You have a strong pull toward becoming the star of the story and the shining knight who saves the day. You do this for the sake of honor and your principles, and you do enjoy the praise you can garner. Your expansive energy means you will be noticed, and it is hard for you to fade into the background, though you probably don't want that. You know how to use your charisma, and your self-confidence looks like supreme confidence to others. As a result, you'll need to be conscious of your actions because you will be seen. You will attract supporters and haters regardless of what you do, so learn to focus on the people who matter to you.

You can reduce the number of haters by making sure you recognize other people's brilliance as well. Maya Angelou had Aries Sun and Leo rising. She shared her life experiences through writing, dance, acting, and song in such a manner that it uplifted others while showing her glory. Be kinder to those who are just learning to shine. The Aries and

Leo amalgamation makes you inherently sunny and plugged into the force of life. You know how to be in each moment and look forward to the future.

Leo rising means that when you reach out to draw in power, fire will answer first. If you need other types of energy, you need to reach farther, focus harder, and be more specific in your request. Your aura and energy are brighter and steadier than most people, so you attract the attention of spirits, deities, and so on. Whether or not showing up so clearly in the other worlds is a gift or a challenge is up to you. Conscious use of this brilliance makes this trait a gift.

Virgo Rising

Your Virgo rising means you don't miss a beat, and you catch every detail. Your Aries disposition toward spontaneity is tempered by the Virgo compulsion to get it all right. This combination also makes you a better judge of character of the probable outcomes of settings you observe. You are good at giving help and advice and you will be sought out by many. The only problem is that you may not know when you need to stop. Keep a close eye on your boundaries and other people's boundaries. If angered, this combination knows how to shred someone with pointed criticism. Hypocrisy and insincerity in yourself and others are big triggers for you.

There is often a conflict between enthusiasm and restraint with this Sun and rising blend. When you rush forward unprepared and make mistakes, you will be particularly harsh in judging yourself. When you find the right balance between your Sun and rising, you can also be a powerful healer of your troubles and those of others. Aries wants to constantly improve and test themselves, and Virgo is excellent at tracking genuine progress. A Virgo rising also bestows a more persistent approach to your daily routine. This in turn means that more of those projects your Aries nature puts into motion will reach completion.

Virgo rising lit up with your Aries fire lets you sense all the details, intricacies, and variations in the energy around you. When you walk into a room or meet someone, reach out and let your instinctive awareness fill you in on what you need to know.

You are really good at finding were the trouble lies in a haunted house or a spooky antique or the deep woods. This knack for noticing what is off-balance is also keen if you do healing work. You also have a flair for abundance or financial magick.

♎

Libra Rising

Libra and Aries are opposite each other in the zodiac, so their energies create a formidable polarity. Your Libra rising likes to focus on other people, and your Aries Sun is all about you. Libra rising is diplomatic and subtle while your Aries Sun prefers directness and can be blunt. You are well aware of all the rules of the world, so you know well why and when you sidestep them or batter them apart. It can bewilder people when you shift easily from one person to another as you swing between the styles of the two signs. You can be elegant and polished just as easily as you can be rebellious and outrageous. Thankfully, these two sides of your makeup are not in disagreement when it comes to your strong sense of life purpose and fairness to self and others.

Libra is more objective and Aries more subjective in considering the meaning of the world around them. When you find the sweet spot between the two perspectives, you have greater clarity on both your goals and how to attain them. Over the years, you are likely to develop an attitude of live and let live. This will lower the stress of this Sun and rising mixture. As long as you get to pursue your happiness and others aren't causing harm, you'll let them be.

Libra rising with an Aries Sun gives a double dose of cardinal energy that is strongly present in your energy. This lends itself to magick related to promises, oaths, and agreements. When you speak with power or listen with intention, those words are inscribed with energy and sent winging forth to become real and manifest. Magick related to bringing peace or justice is favored by this combination. Libra rising lit with Aries fire is adept at casting glamouries and spells of beauty or charisma.

Scorpio Rising

Your Aries Sun already makes you hotblooded, but when you add in the Scorpio rising, it takes it up to incandescent. You often come across as being aggressive and uncompromising when in your mind you are just protecting yourself or following your personal code. Intense emotions are your norm, though you are good at hiding them when you want to. You give off an attractive vibe that draws people to you like moths to flame. This is true for romantic, platonic, and business connections. Try to give clear messages to the people in your life for their sake and your own. Unless you are emoting strongly and obviously, you can be hard to read. Pride in the right amount—not too little and not too much—is an essential part of your personality.

You have a strong impact on people. You will be remembered by people even if it is a short encounter. You have a tremendous amount of energy and the ability to affect the world around you. You would prefer to be in charge, and even when you are not officially in the role of leader, you help shape decisions. You love to dig for secrets and ferret out the truth, but be careful, lest you become overly suspicious of everyone—including yourself.

Scorpio rising makes your energy capable of pushing through most energetic barriers. You can dissolve illusion or bring down wards or shields and see through to the truth. Road opening and obstacle clearing come naturally to this combination. You have a talent for doing cleansings and banishing negative energies or spirits. With proper training, you would do well at divine embodiment and trance work. It is important that you do regular cleansing work for yourself. You are likely to end up doing messy work, and you do not have a nonstick aura.

Sagittarius Rising

You come across as idealistic, philosophical, and fun loving. You love talking about the big picture and a world with more liberty. Your Aries Sun indicates you will also fight for the things you espouse. You love learning about different cultures and communities, and if the opportunity for travel arises, you will benefit greatly from the experiences. When you get excited about something, you feel the need to share it with everyone. You are good as a teacher, salesperson, promoter, clergy, or any task that involves sharing the best points about a topic. You give the impression of being informed on whatever subject you talk about, whether or not you are informed.

You are healthier if you keep physically active. Motion is life for someone with a Sagittarius rising. Your need for activity and novelty can make you the life of the party, but you can be too much at times. You swing easily from refined discourse to crudeness, so be mindful of your audience and companions. Don't rely on reading the room; get a direct confirmation from those present as to whether or not they are comfortable. Your Aries Sun's desire to be a warrior will probably emerge as work toward cultural change.

Sagittarius rising gives you a double dose of fire but adds finesse and flexibility to your Aries fire. Your energy is well suited to calling upon and working with divine beings. Offerings you make to deities, ancestors, spirits, and so on are noticed quickly.

This is because you can push your energy and intentions into objects with ease. You have a talent for rituals and spells that call forth creativity, wisdom, and freedom. This combination gives access to lots of energy, but you can crash hard when you run out. Stop before you are tired.

♑

Capricorn Rising

Both Aries and Capricorn really need and want to do things their way. Your sense of independence and autonomy are central to how you navigate your life. That said, there are more differences between the two signs than similarities. Your Aries Sun believes if they want something strongly enough, all things are possible. Your Capricorn rising is pragmatic and aware of all the obstacles to be overcome. These two perspectives must come to terms with each other or take turns. This tension is never resolved, is always revisited, and will be the source of great ideas and personal growth. Your Capricorn rising gives you more patience and perseverance than is normal for an Aries. With Aries Sun, your energy wants to shift from target to target, but the Capricorn rising makes you fixate on a goal until it is reached.

This rising tends to make you appear colder and more restrained and hides some of your fiery nature. Some people may think you project haughtiness, while others may view you as radiating strong self-confidence. When you are not doing well emotionally, it is important to continue to reach out to people. You may yearn for isolating yourself until you feel better, but that will tend to lengthen your melancholy.

Capricorn rising creates an aura and energy field that is slow to come up to speed, but it has amazing momentum once fully activated. Make it your habit to do some sort of energy work or meditative warm-up before engaging in witchcraft. You may be underestimating your abilities because you are not fully up to speed before you begin your work. Try working with crystals, stones, and even geographic features like mountains as your magick blends well with them. Your Aries fire awakens the cardinal earth in these. Your rituals and spells benefit from having a structure and plan of action. You can still be spontaneous because having a sense of where you are headed in your work gives you more liberty to act in the moment.

♒

Aquarius Rising

This combination is freewheeling, forward thinking, and always on the move. There is a love of the eccentric, and if the level of excitement drops below your threshold, you move on to the next thing. Much of your Sun sign's energy is redirected into curiosity by your rising. You view the world at an angle, live outside the box, and can find solutions to problems others can't see from their vantage point. You also have a talent for making sense of technical matters.

The Aries aspiration to lead is still present, but the Aquarius rising prefers to win people over rather than using power alone to win. Friendliness and enthusiasm can be one of your superpowers. When there is a crisis, you stay coolheaded and power through until the emergency is resolved. You are nimble and quick to adapt as circumstances change. You tend to gravitate toward professions and organizations where you serve the public good. Your Aries warrior energy is redirected by the Aquarius rising toward the good of your community and society. You are at a loss when you don't have enough to do. This is when self-doubts start bubbling up. Search until you find activities or practices that let you relax when you are not up to your ears in tasks.

Aquarius rising helps Aries interact with other people's energy with more detachment and objectivity. This smooths the way in group ritual and makes divination clearer and more honest. Witchcraft focused on calling inspiration, creating community, and personal transformation are supported by this combination. Visualization can play an important role in your magick and meditations. If you aren't particularly good at visualization, then focus your gaze on objects on your altar or other symbols related to your work. Aquarius rising is gifted at turning ideas onto reality.

Pisces Rising

The tremendous Aries energy to get up and go fuels a love of the art, music, the mysteries of the world, and fantasy in all its forms. You can be immensely creative and have a powerful capacity for imagination and altered states. One of the keys to being happy and effective in your life is to be conscious of how much you are affected by your environment. Your Aries Sun would like to pretend you steer your own course in the world, but your Pisces rising connects you to the tides and influences of all the world. You have a good deal of empathy and psychism, so it is best to acknowledge that and learn how to manage it.

You can be thought of as a daydreamer, as someone easily distracted during a conversation, but the truth is you are tuned in to more than just what is happening in the physical world. You give love and affection easily and in ways that truly show you care. Although being connected at a deep level with the world is a gift, it can also make it more likely that others will take advantage of you. With time and experience, you can blend the fire of Aries and the water of Pisces to become truly wise and at ease in the world.

Pisces rising brings a union of the last sign with the first sign, which completes the wheel of the zodiac. Your power as a witch flows when you do magick to open the gates to the other worlds. You have a special gift for creating sacred space and blessing places. You can do astral travel, hedge riding, and soul travel in all forms with some training and practice. Pay attention to your dreams, both while sleeping or daydreaming, and keep notes for guidance on your path. Music, chanting, and dance also fuel your witchcraft.

A DISH FIT FOR AN ARIES:
SWEET-AND-SOUR SALMON FOR SUCCESS

Dawn Aurora Hunt

✳ ✳ ✳

This recipe features a lightly marinated salmon steak quickly seared then put over brown rice with wilted kale, sliced cucumbers, sliced onions, cilantro, and topped with kimchi and a bit of spicey mayo.

Quick and energizing, this meal comes together in no time—perfect for the Aries witch who wants to make the most out of their time and achieve their goals. Kimchi is fermented cabbage well known in Korea for being nutrient rich, flavorful, and spicy. It holds magical properties of the element of fire and is ruled by Mars, like Aries, which helps one get up and go toward their goals. This dish also features rice and kale, two powerhouse prosperity foods.

Note: If your diet precludes you from eating fish, you can easily substitute the salmon for firm tofu and follow the same instructions. To easily make this recipe gluten-free, choose tamari or another gluten-free soy sauce.

Ingredients:

- 4 salmon steaks, skin on, about 6 ounces each
- ½ large cucumber
- ¼ white onion
- 2 cups chopped kale (stems removed)
- 2 cups brown rice cooked to package instructions
- 2–4 tablespoons kimchi (more if desired)
- Chopped cilantro for garnish
- *For the marinade:*
    - ¼ cup sesame oil, plus 2 tablespoons for cooking
    - ¼ cup soy sauce
    - 1 teaspoon rice vinegar
    - 2 tablespoons brown sugar
    - 1 tablespoon fresh grated ginger
    - 1 tablespoon fresh grated garlic
    - Juice from ½ lime
- *For the spicy mayo:*
    - ½ cup mayonnaise
    - 1 tablespoon siracha
    - Juice from one lime

Directions:

In a large container or bowl, make the marinade by whisking together the sesame oil, soy sauce, rice vinegar, brown sugar, ginger, garlic, and lime juice. Place the salmon steaks in the container, coat with marinade, and cover the container. Let the salmon marinate for thirty to sixty minutes at room temperature. Meanwhile, slice the cucumber and onion into paper-thin slices and set aside. Next, whisk together all the spicy mayo ingredients and place in the refrigerator to set. Heat two tablespoons of sesame oil to medium-high heat in a large skillet. In a medium saucepot, bring one cup of water to a soft boil, reduce the heat, and place the kale in the pot. Cover and let steam about three minutes. Remove from heat as to not overheat, drain the water, and cover until ready to serve. Gently place salmon steaks, skin side down, in the hot pan. Cook for three minutes. Gently flip the salmon over and cook for an additional three minutes or until desired internal temperature. For each serving, place half a cup of cooked rice in a bowl, top with wilted kale, and then top the kale with a cooked salmon steak. Top with sliced cucumbers, onions, kimchi, and cilantro. Drizzle spicy mayo on top and serve immediately.

RECHARGING AND SELF-CARE: WHEN THE FIRE HAS FIZZLED

Diotima Mantineia

There are two common reasons for an Aries witch to need a recharge—they have burned themselves out, or someone has quenched their fire. Either way, a tired Aries is one whose fire is burning low, which means it's time for some rest and relaxation.

Wait, what?! Aries, resting and relaxing?! Nah. We're more likely to keep going until we drop. Which not only isn't fun, but is also kind of humiliating. So, let's look at some ways to recharge that don't involve languidly reclining on the fainting couch like some Victorian maiden or dropping in our tracks from sheer exhaustion.

Burnout is probably the most common of the two scenarios for an Aries. Our enthusiasm for life in general and particularly for getting things done, for making things happen in the world, set us up for this.

A classic burnout scenario for me is at festivals and conventions. Enthusiasm is a trademark of Aries, and my enthusiasms lead me from classroom to ritual space to social events and back to the classroom again. Sleep? Why would I want to do that? Until, of course, the inevitable happens, and my body demands rest in a way I can't ignore.

Over the years I've been attending these events, I've learned some tricks for managing my energy. Here are my Aries-focused tricks of the trade for getting through an event without burning out. They aren't just for events, either. They are useful anytime we are at risk of burnout.

Feeding the Fire That's Burned Out

The key is learning to manage your inner fire—your enthusiasm and energy will only take you so far before the fuel runs out. Here's how to make sure you have the energy you need to do what you want.

🔥 First, plan ahead and plan around. I set my expectations early on, deciding what's important, what I most want to experience at this event. Are there certain presenters I really want to see? Will a lot of friends be there I want to catch up with? Are there certain rituals I know I definitely want to attend? How much sleep do I know I need, and when will I get it? Knowing my priorities helps me plan my free playtimes around them. (This is true for your daily life, too!)

🔥 The second step is writing the priorities down. Aries usually prefer to be spontaneous and tend to balk at anything resembling a schedule because it might limit our options to go wherever our impulses in the moment take us. But we learn early on that plans can be helpful, and there's no rule that says you can't make planning fun and creative! Go ahead and get out the crayons and markers and oversized sticky notes you can put up on the wall, or play with a fancy online calendar if that's what works best for you. Just get those priorities solidified in paper or pixels so you don't lose sight of what's most important when you're in the middle of all the exciting and distracting possibilities around you.

🔥 Cleansing, warding, and blessing are some of the most important tools in the witch's tool kit. Don't leave your daily practices at home. I have travel versions of any magical materia and tools I use. Consciously managing your personal energy and the energy of your space is key to preventing burnout. I've found that Aries witches tend to overemphasize the cleansing and warding at the expense of taking time for blessings. But particularly when you are trying to avoid or recover from burnout, the blessing part is crucial to restoring your power. Take nourishing baths with restorative herbs or potions, light a candle or two, and repeat whatever invocations/affirmations/prayers bring you to that inner recharging station where you can receive the restorative energies and blessings the universe gifts to you.

🔥 Ground into the land. Maybe you work with the spirits of the land; maybe you just try to sense the resonance of the planet and tune your personal energy to it. But no matter which approach we take, the Earth holds us all, provides for us, and offers both a source of magical power and a repository for excess energy. The resonance and the spirits of the land change from place to place, so paying attention to that is important when we travel—even just from home to work, but especially at a magically oriented event. Offerings help with this. I'm sure I've left a number of travelers scratching their heads as they saw me scattering a little bit of cornmeal and pouring water onto whatever uncovered patch of earth I could find in a hotel parking lot. The spirits of the land often seem surprised, too—it's rare for humans to acknowledge them—but definitely appreciative!

Listen to your body and honor its needs. We Aries often have this underlying conviction that all the energy in the universe is available to us at any time. And maybe it should be (I wouldn't argue with that!), but our body will continue to prove to us that it's not. Rest, food, and water are not optional. Hot baths with relaxing and restorative herbs such as lavender, chamomile, nettles, and rosemary will help, particularly if you bless the herbs and water as you are preparing the bath.

Feeding the Fire That's Been Quenched

Sometimes your fire may go out because of an emotional setback of some kind, which may or may not be accompanied by stressful outer circumstances. Heavy emotional weather will often put out your inner fire, and it will need to be rebuilt, not just managed. When your fire has been doused, there's not only an emotional component, but often a sense of spiritual disconnection that needs to be addressed as well. So, while the above advice about cleansing and blessing and connecting with the land still holds, with an emotional situation that's weighing you down, there are other approaches you'll want to explore.

If the emotional upheaval is serious, then connecting with a therapist or a friend who will help you work through it may be the first step. But if you're just feeling blah, or you'd rather do something now and talk about it later, here are some ideas:

🔥 Find some actual fire—a candle, a bonfire, or even sunshine—and bask in it. Envision the dancing flames sending energy to you, to every cell of your body. Feel its healing warmth.

🔥 Get moving! Exercise is restorative for Aries— we are happiest when we are in motion. I love to dance, so if I'm feeling down, I'll put on a dance playlist I know will be hard to resist and let loose. If dancing isn't your thing, try a walk outdoors, a session of yoga or tai chi, or playing whatever sport you enjoy; this will help relight that fire.

🔥 Make sure your environment is helping and not hindering you. If you haven't done a home clearing and blessing recently, this would be a good time. Open the windows to whatever extent the weather allows. Light some candles. Buy some flowers and think of them as an offering to yourself.

🔥 Freshen up your altar! First, remove anything that isn't an active part of your current practices/ workings/offerings. Old stuff hanging around is a magnet for unhealthy energy. Launder any cloths you use, dust, and, of course, as you're tearing the altar apart, you'll want to focus on disinviting any inharmonious energies that have gathered around it. As you are putting it back together, connect with and welcome any spirits or deities you work with regularly. Now your space is working with you to heal and restore your body and mind.

 Get together with some friends and have fun. When we're down, a party, a visit to a favorite local pub or music venue, or just hanging out with people we care about and who care about us will go a long way toward restoring us. Ideally, your friends will be witches, too, because then you can work some magic together. Back in the days I was working as a waitress, I had a witchy coworker/friend, and often we'd set an intention for our shift to make as many people smile as possible. We'd weave our energy together and think about all the things in our lives that made us happy, made us smile. Then we'd make sure to take some of that energy with us to every table. You don't have to be a server to work this spell, and it's amazing what a difference it can make when two or more witches work it together. Depending on where you're going and how much work you and your friends are willing to put into it, you can create a sigil to draw on a table using water or in the air wherever you go, or have a charged oil you all wear, and if you are at a place where there is a candle on the table, put some of that energy in the candle, and leave it burning even after you leave. Joy is contagious, and you'll find that if you spread some around, it will come back to you multiplied.

Your Opposite Sign Can Help

In the great circle of the zodiac, the signs that are opposite each other have similar lessons to learn, but they approach those lessons from different angles. Whenever you are feeling blocked, stressed, burned out, or just blah, often you can find a cure for what ails you by invoking the strengths of your opposite sign, Libra. For example:

🔥 Aries is all about individuality and being able to go it alone. Libra reminds us of the joys of relationship and that others can have our back, if we let them.

🔥 Aries tends to confront problems with great courage and steely determination. Libra reminds us that some problems only need a bit of time and diplomacy to disappear.

🔥 Aries puts lots of energy into creating, making something in the world. Libra reminds us to appreciate what has been created, to relax and take in the beauty that surrounds us.

But the main lesson we can learn from Libra is finding balance. Aries witches will enthusiastically pour energy into their spells and other projects, and if we aren't paying attention to how much energy we are expending versus how much we are taking in, we exhaust ourselves.

Magic is an energy-intensive pursuit. Sometimes it will energize us, sometimes it will drain us, sometimes it just shifts our personal energy into different realms, so when we emerge from a magical space, we need to shift our subtle bodies back into resonance with ordinary reality, like a dog shaking its fur back into place.

Aries witches in the throes of enthusiasm (as we often are) can pour a tremendous amount of energy into a ritual, or spell, or any pet project before we realize that maybe we've overdone it. Reminding ourselves to take the time we need to tune in and recharge will ensure that we have the energy we need to fully engage with life and magic in our inimitable Aries way.

A SPELL FOR PHYSICAL FITNESS/ACCEPTANCE

By Michael Cabrera

This spell is perfect for an Aries trying to tap into their Sun sign energy to get in better shape or even just to become better caretakers of their body, no matter their level of fitness. Do this spell before starting a new exercise routine or generally as a body-positive working. It's great to do on your birthday. The concept is to make uplifting affirmations to your body as a proud starting point to whatever health-focused endeavor you have planned.

You will need:

+ 1 red candle
+ Dragon's Blood oil
+ Carnelian
+ A mirror (optional)

Instructions:

Be fully clothed when starting this spell.

Dress the red candle with Dragon's Blood oil. Place the carnelian between you and the candle. A mirror nearby that you can fully see yourself in is helpful, but not necessary.

Light the candle and say, "By my birthright, I invoke Aries."

Draw a pentagram above the candle with your dominant finger while saying, "I invoke the initiative, power, beauty, strength, and worth of Aries." Envision the pentagram glowing fiery red with the characteristics of a self-actualized Aries—a pioneer who is courageous, disciplined, and confident. Imagine that Aries having already met the personal goals you are setting out for.

With the attention of the pentagram, mindfully undress yourself as much as you are comfortable. Notice what your body looks like and how it makes you feel. Allow yourself to feel whatever comes without judgment. Take one deep breath, and on exhalation, expel that feeling away, allowing yourself to feel hollow and ready to be filled with power.

Then, in one deep breath, fill yourself with the Aries pentagram you drew above the candle, absorbing the traits you've envisioned. Imagine the pentagram shining warmly into your throat then up to your head. As you exhale, picture it descending to your perineum, where it is stored as energy for your goals. When this is accomplished, announce, "I am an Aries!"

Displaying your body to the carnelian, confidently proclaim, "Behold, the body of an Aries, with the initiative, power, beauty, and strength of an Aries. A body worthy of being called 'Aries.' I am impressively made!"

Observe your body. Notice your perfection in the perspective of the words you've just used. Allow yourself to feel proud.

Show various parts of your body to the carnelian and say the "Behold" statement with the name of each body part in place of "body." For example, "Behold, the belly of an Aries…" or, "Behold, the biceps of an Aries…" or even, "Behold, the sex of an Aries…" Do this with the parts of you that you feel good about, but especially do this with the parts of you that you typically feel negative about.

When you have finished, make a promise to your body: "I promise to take care of you, to respect you, to believe in you, and to exalt you as you deserve."

Extinguish the candle.

Carry the carnelian with you, especially when doing anything in relation to your fitness goals. Every time you think about it or during rest times, intone, "Behold, the body of an Aries. I am impressively made." You can also say this for specific body parts when you are working on them.

DON'T BLAME IT ON YOUR SUN SIGN

Diotima Mantineia

In my years as an astrologer, I've had plenty of people tell me, "I'm not like a [their Sun sign] at all!" Some of them are genuinely puzzled, others just want to tell me why they don't believe in astrology. I have standard replies I use in social situations, but when it's a client I'm reading for, I get to go a bit deeper. And inevitably I find that they are, in fact, like their Sun sign. They may not show it because other planetary placements in their chart modulate or even repress its expression. But I've never read for anyone who didn't, at some level, resonate with their Sun sign.

Mostly, this is a good thing. But every sign has its shadow side, and it can be easy to resonate with that as well. I don't believe the planets *make* us do anything. But they certainly can impel us toward certain behaviors. So, it's important for an Aries witch to know the pitfalls Aries are prone to so we can avoid falling into them. I have a good understanding of Aries' pitfalls, not only from my own experience and my Aries clients, but from my father and stepmother as well.

For an Aries, Love Is Always Young. And Loud.

When my dad (an Aries) turned ninety-two, he had been widowed and unhappy for a couple of years. Then he met Catherine (eighty-nine, also an Aries), and the two of them fell head over heels in love with each other. Their relationship was not one of quiet companionship, as might be expected from people that age. In a typically Aries way, their relationship was full of passionate enthusiasm and declarations of undying love. I lived only a few minutes away and loved them both, so we all spent a fair amount of time together. It was a great opportunity to study pure Aries relationship and family dynamics.

Despite any declarations of undying love, when two or more Aries are gathered together, someone's going to start yelling sooner or later, and our family was no exception. Aries really like to yell. We yell when we're angry, but we often yell anytime we just want to make a point or need to drain off some emotional energy. We seem to believe that loud = effective (though it's really only effective in getting attention and/ or driving people away). Sometimes our yelling is just an expression of excitement or approval, but often it's a crude form of setting boundaries or manipulating a situation.

Dad was a straightforward yeller. When he was irritated or frustrated, he'd start raising his voice, and the volume would continue to increase until the situation resolved itself. Catherine, though, was a much more strategic yeller. She would wait, then jump in at full volume at the most effective time, taking the object of her ire (usually my dad) by surprise. She was so effective (and he was so much in love) that sometimes she even managed to shut him up.

Reining It In

Watching them helped me realize that, while yelling may be a good way of letting off steam, it's not terribly effective in changing whatever situation triggered the yelling. The classic Aries temper tantrum is perfected around age two. As we grow up, most of us learn to suppress our tantrums, since they are not socially acceptable and are often counterproductive, but we can still fall into the tantrum trap when we're angry. That's because suppression doesn't work well with Aries. What works is expanding our perspective through what people who regularly deal with crisis situations call "situational awareness."

A quick temper is part of the Aries soul. We respond to any perceived injustice or interference in our plans with lightning speed. We run toward danger instead of away from it and will take a stand to defend whatever we think needs defending. Since keeping a lid on our temper is not something we do well, we need to learn to channel it in productive ways.

Remember what I mentioned earlier about anger being a red flag? Well, yelling is a red flag that you're probably already angry and moving into temper tantrum territory. Though it takes some training and practice, it's possible to learn how to let those red flags trigger a shift into situational awareness. Instead of yelling or lashing out, we can immediately redirect our awareness to assess our surroundings and determine the best action to take in response. Training in any practices that help develop situational awareness will help us turn our explosive tempers into a tool instead of a bludgeon.

The practices that worked for me were meditation, magic, dance, and martial arts. Meditation and magical training helped me unwind some of the internal processes that were interfering with clear awareness. Dance and martial arts helped me become more present in and learn to listen to my body.

Situational awareness requires awareness of your own internal state (you're part of the situation), your body, and its location within the space around you. It also requires awareness of other people around you, assessing, as far as possible, their intentions, emotional state, and likely actions, and of any threats or advantages in your environment. It's learning to use the space between a stimulus and your response that turns a quick temper into a fast and—most importantly—appropriate reaction to whatever angered you. It turns anger into fuel for action instead of a destructive conflagration.

Practicing when you're not angry or upset is the key to learning to do this well. Because situational awareness is not an intellectual activity—it can't be, in a situation where an immediate response is required. We have to train our minds and bodies to pay attention and be ready to respond faster than we can think.

When you were learning to drive, did your instructor tell you that you should turn into a spin instead of away from it, and not hit the brake? More than likely, they took you someplace where you could safely practice how to get out of a spin, because just knowing that information intellectually doesn't really help when your car's spinning out of control. But if you train your body and brain through practice, when the situation is real, you'll react almost before you realize what is happening.

Martial arts such as Krav Maga and kung fu offer excellent training in situational awareness. Tai chi is also a martial art and a good choice for those who prefer something less physically taxing. But you can practice and develop this skill on your own. Here are some ideas on how to get started:

1. Practice mindfulness, a quality that is innate in humans—our ability to be present in the moment.

Our minds are often jumping around from the past to the future, and back again. Make a habit of bringing your attention fully back into the present at regular intervals.

2. As you move through your day, take a moment to identify what's around you when you enter a new space. Whether you're going into a meeting, or the grocery store, or just getting back home, expand your awareness. Where are the entrances and exits, how are people situated or moving around, what's the general vibe of the place?

3. Monitor and identify your emotions and thoughts. Not just, "Oh, I'm in a bad mood." What mood is that? Are you depressed? Resentful? Angry? If you're in a great mood, notice what caused it. What were you thinking about? It's as important to be aware of your inner processes as it is your external environment.

Regular meditators easily develop an Observer, a part of their mind that watches what's going on without reacting. If you're dead set against having a regular meditation practice, you can still work on developing your Observer by asking for help from whatever spirits or deities you work with regularly, or by creating an amulet or talisman to remind you to check in with yourself and your environment.

Aries witches have an advantage in learning situational awareness, because as witches, we actively work on training our psychic abilities. Aries' natural intuitive abilities can be trained to stay running in the background and alert us to changes in our internal or external environments without dragging us into states of hypervigilance or anxiety.

I'm still working on situational awareness. It's a life-long learning process that involves not only learning new skills but overcoming innate impulses and past conditioning. It's an extremely useful ability for an Aries to develop, and well worth pursuing.

Another insight I got from watching Dad and Catherine is that Aries are incorrigibly blunt and honest. It's not that we won't ever lie, it's just that we aren't very good at it, and we'd rather lay out exactly what we're thinking, and then butt heads over it if necessary.

In fact, Aries enjoy butting heads sometimes. I remember one Christmas Eve with Dad and Catherine when Dad and I got into a rather loud argument about what was needed to get the fire going properly in the fireplace. An important point of Yuletide strategy, to be sure! But we were just playing around, and we both knew it. The insults we were throwing back and forth were not barbed and could even be considered funny—at least by another Aries.

If this had happened at the larger Christmas Day family gathering, there would have been handwringing among other family members and attempts to broker peace. But when I looked over at Catherine, she was watching us and smiling. Eventually, we all started laughing, Dad got the fire going, and we moved on to singing carols.

Tact is not one of Aries' strong points. It's a learned skill that may still be somewhat lacking even after ninety-two years on the planet, as Dad discovered one evening when he spoke to Catherine in a remarkably tactless way that she definitely did not appreciate. I had never seen Catherine really angry before, and I watched in admiration as she told him, in no uncertain terms, exactly what she thought of his behavior and exactly what the consequences would be (brutal) if he ever spoke to her like that again.

The stunned look on his face was priceless, and he quickly backed off and apologized, which in itself was somewhat unusual. Normally, he'd take the typically Aries tactic of defending his position until everyone else was exhausted and gave in. Catherine, in her crone's wisdom, taught me a lot about setting boundaries, and taught Dad a few much-needed lessons as well.

Aries' primary mission is individuation—the development of the self. While there are many cultural and religious strictures wrapped around the concepts of self and ego, the witch need not feel bound by them. After all, just by being witches, we've already overthrown more than a few conventions. But when you overthrow something, it's important to consider what you want to replace it with.

Aries tend to plow through obstacles, then move on to the next thing, leaving others to pick up the pieces. But self-development and individuation require taking responsibility for your actions, and taking a stand for what you believe in. It means thinking carefully about your place in the world, your personal values, your deepest desires, and the source of your magic.

Individuation does not translate to self-centeredness. Quite the opposite, in fact. It requires our full participation in life and in relationships. But healthy relationships require two (or more) people who are reasonably healthy themselves, and a healthy individual is one who is working toward fulfilling the promise of their soul.

Individuation means becoming, essentially, the best you can be. I'll take a look at how an Aries witch can pursue that goal in the chapter Better Every Day.

Water Grounding Ritual for Fiery Witches

Catalina Castells

Let me tell you a story. When I was a young witch, I met an Italian astrologer named Giovanni. We were in the same witchy networking group in Philadelphia back in the day. He very kindly offered to do my natal chart for me and took down my birth information. About two weeks later, I received a phone message from him demanding that I call him immediately. He sounded concerned. So, I called him back when I got home from work, and he sounded relieved. "I was worried you might have spontaneously combusted!" he said.

You see, I have absolutely no earth signs in my chart and only one water sign. I'm all air and fire, with an Aries Sun to ignite the mix. He gave me all sorts of useful information, but the one I've actually used the most was this: "Don't bother trying to ground with earth. Instead, use the water. Take a bath or a shower or have a long cool drink of water. For you, it will work better."

Over the years, this has served me well. While I actually can ground in a more earthy way that I learned through years of practicing with my coven, I've developed a ritual I do for myself when I'm over-wrought or struggling to ground. This ritual works whether or not you have earth in your chart.

I start with a special candle. Maybe I like the scent. Maybe I drew some sigils on it. Maybe it's a gift from a loved one. It just needs to feel special. I light it and set my intentions. After all, it's the intent that matters most! I then draw a bath or warm up my shower. Both work equally well. The candle is within sight to use as a focus if my mind starts to wander. If I'm taking a bath, I might use a soothing bubble bath or salts, like vanilla or lavender.

Stepping into the bath or shower, I take three deep breaths to center myself. Then I let all of the ungrounded energy bubble up inside of me. If I'm sad, I cry. If I'm angry, I growl or rant. When I've really brought it all up to the surface, I begin to release it to water. I ask water, out loud if I am comfortable doing so, to take the energy and drain it down into the land beneath me. Water is a conduit, like a grounding wire, that I use to connect with Earth. It's like an ambassador between fiery me and the distant-feeling Earth.

The magic, for me, happens at the drain. As the water from the bath or shower exits the vessel, and the last few drops roll down the drain, I step out and extinguish the candle, thanking all four elements for supporting my work. Before I dry off, I affirm my relationship with them.

I am Air.
I am Fire.
I am Water.
I am Earth.
I am FREE.

POSTCARD FROM AN ARIES WITCH

Danielle Blackwood

While having Sun, Moon, and Mars in Aries has been a lifelong lesson in cultivating patience, learning to pick my battles wisely, and counting to ten before jumping in with both feet, it's also come with its gifts. And as I've honed these gifts over the years, I've realized that they have been an integral part of my magical practice and my experience as a witch for more than three decades. So, what inherent Aries gifts can be magical allies?

Aries teaches us how to take the initiative and to break new ground. Like all forms of creativity, magic usually always carries some sense of risk, a turning point where we take a deep breath, strike the match, and step out of our comfort zone to create something new. No sign embraces new beginnings and embodies that "feel the fear and do it anyway" sensibility like Aries.

And while occasionally we can burn our fingers, Aries medicine is the life-giving, revitalizing tonic that gives us the courage to blaze new trails, build self-confidence, and take action. This willingness to take risks and embrace new experiences is woven into Aries' cosmic DNA. I would not have the breadth and depth of insight I have as an Aries witch at this stage in my life had I not gone down a few roads that angels would fear to tread.

As the first sign, Aries is the spark that begins new life. The first step on the Hero's Journey. It is the irrepressible force of rebirth after winter. It carries with it the instinct to become, and to self-actualize. Working with Aries as a magical ally can help us set something in motion to harness the fire of our passion and direct it through willpower into manifestation.

And finally, mindset is an integral part of magic. If it weren't for the Aries gifts of optimism, enthusiasm, and audacity, I might never have written my books, started my practice, raised my son on my own, or gone back to school in my thirties. I am grateful for my impetuous Aries spirit, which over the years has become less an out-of-control wildfire, and more a steady flame born of stories gathered through a lifetime of adventure.

• SPIRIT OF ARIES GUIDANCE RITUAL •

Ivo Dominguez, Jr.

The signs are more than useful constructs in astrology or categories for describing temperaments, they are also powerful and complicated spiritual entities. So, what is meant when we say that a sign is a spirit? I often describe the signs of the zodiac as the twelve forms of human wisdom and folly. The signs are twelve styles of human consciousness, which also means that the signs are well-developed group minds and egregores. Think on the myriad of people over thousands of years who have poured energy into the constructs of the signs through intentional visualization and study. Moreover, the lived experience of each person as one of the signs is deposited into the group minds and egregores of their sign; they are ensouled. Every Aries who has ever lived or is living contributes to the spirit of Aries.

The signs have a composite nature that allows them to exist in many forms on multiple planes of reality at once. In addition to the human contribution to their existence, the spirits of the signs are made from inputs from all living beings in our world whether they are made of dense matter or spiritual substances. These vast and ancient thoughtforms that became group minds and then egregores are also vessels that can be used by divine beings to communicate with humans as well. The spirits of the signs can manifest themselves as small as a sprite or larger than the Earth. The shape and the magnitude of the spirit of Aries emerging before you will depend on who you are and how and why you call upon them.

Purpose and Use

This ritual will make it possible to commune with the spirit of Aries. The form that the spirit will take will be different each time you perform the ritual. What appears will be determined by what you are looking for and your state of mind and soul. The process for preparing yourself for the ritual will do you good as well. Exploring your circumstances, motivations and intentions is a valuable experience whether or not you are performing this ritual.

If you have a practical problem you are trying to solve or an obstacle that must be overcome, the spirit of Aries may have useful advice. If you are try-ing to better understand who you are and what you are striving to accomplish, then the spirit of Aries can be your mentor. Should you have a need to recharge yourself or flush out stale energy, you can use this ritual to reconnect with a strong clear cur-rent of power. This energy can be used for magickal empowerment, physical vitality, or healing or redi-rected for spell work. If you are charging objects or magickal implements with Aries energy, this ritual can be used for this purpose as well.

Timing for the Ritual

The prevailing astrological conditions have an impact on how you experience a ritual, the type and amount of power available, and the outcomes of the work. If you decide you want to go deeper in your stud-ies of astrology, you'll find many techniques to pick the best day and time for your ritual. Thankfully, the ritual to meet the spirit of your sign does not require exact timing or perfect astrological conditions. This ritual depends upon your inner connection to your Sun sign, so it is not as reliant on the external celes-tial conditions as some other rituals. Each of us has worlds within ourselves, which include inner land-scapes and inner skies. Your birth chart, and the sky that it depicts, burns brightest within you. Although not required, you can improve the effectiveness of this ritual if you use any of the following simple guidelines for favorable times:

- When the Moon or the Sun is in Aries
- When Mars is in Aries
- On Tuesdays, the day of Mars, and even better at dawn, which is its planetary hour
- When Mars is in Capricorn, where it is exalted

Materials and Setup

The following is a description of the physical objects that will make it easier to perform this ritual. Don't worry if you don't have all of them; as in a pinch, you need no props. However, the physical objects will help to anchor the energy and your mental focus.

You will need:

- A printout of your birth chart
- A table to serve as an altar

+ A chair if you want to sit during the ritual
+ A candle, ideally a red one but any color will do. For fire safety, it should be in glass and on a plate or tray.
+ An assortment of items for the altar that corresponds with Aries or Mars. For example, a carnelian or a red jasper, cayenne pepper or peppercorns, and a red flower.
+ A pad and a pen or chalk and a small blackboard, or something else you can use to draw a glyph

Before beginning the ritual, you may wish to copy the ritual invocations onto paper or bookmark this chapter and bring the book into the ritual. I find that the process of writing out the invocation, whether handwritten or typed, helps to forge a better connection with the words and their meaning. If possible, put the altar table in the center of your space, and if not, then as close to due east as you can manage. Light the candle and place it on the altar. Put the printout of your birth chart on the altar to one side of the candle and arrange the items you have selected to anchor the Aries and Mars energy around it. To the other side of the candle, place the pad and pen. Make sure you turn off your phone, close the door, close the curtains, or do whatever else is needed to prevent distractions.

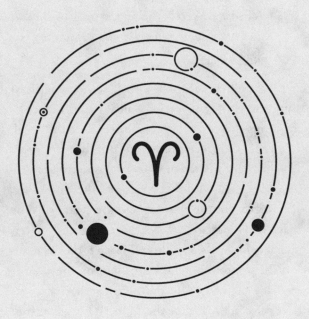

Ritual to Meet the Spirit of Your Sign

You may stand or be seated—whichever is most comfortable for you. Begin by focusing on your breathing. When you pay attention to the process of breathing, you become more aware of your body, the flow of your life energy, and the balance between conscious and unconscious actions. After you have done so for about a minute, it is time to shift into fourfold breathing. This consists of four phases: inhaling, lungs full, exhaling, and lungs empty. You count to keep time so that each of the four phases is of equal duration. Try a count of four or five in your first efforts. Depending on your lungs and how fast you count, you will need to adjust the number higher or lower. When you hold your breath, hold it with your belly muscles, not your throat. When you hold your breath in fourfold breathing, your throat should feel relaxed. Be gentle and careful with yourself if you have asthma, high blood pressure, are late in pregnancy, or have any other condition that may have an impact on your breathing and blood pressure. In general, if there are difficulties, they arise during the lungs' full or empty phases because of holding them by clenching the throat or compressing the lungs. The empty and the full lungs should be held by the position of the diaphragm, and the air passages left open. After one to three minutes of fourfold breathing, you can return to your normal breathing pattern.

Now, close your eyes and move your center of consciousness down into the middle of your chest. Proceed with grounding and centering, dropping and opening, shifting into the alpha state, or whatever practice you use to reach the state of mind that supports ritual work. Then gaze deeply inside yourself and see a fire. The flames can be in a hearth, a bonfire, on a torch, or whatever feels right to you. Look at the dancing flames, hear the crackling, and feel the warmth. Reach out from that central fire and awaken all the places and spaces within you that are of Aries. When you feel ready, open your eyes.

Zodiac Casting

If you are seated, stand if you are able and face the east. Slowly read this invocation aloud, putting some energy into your words. As you read it, slowly turn counterclockwise so that you come full circle when you reach the last line. Another option is to hold your hand over your head and trace the counterclockwise circle of the zodiac with your finger.

> *I call forth the twelve to join me in this rite.*
> *I call forth Aries and the power of courage.*
> *I call forth Taurus and the power of stability.*
> *I call forth Gemini and the power of versatility.*
> *I call forth Cancer and the power of protection.*
> *I call forth Leo and the power of the will.*
> *I call forth Virgo and the power of discernment.*
> *I call forth Libra and the power of harmony.*
> *I all forth Scorpio and the power of renewal.*
> *I call forth Sagittarius and the power of vision.*
> *I call forth Capricorn and the power of responsibility.*
> *I call forth Aquarius and the power of innovation.*
> *I call forth Pisces and the power of compassion.*
> *The power of the twelve is here.*
> *Blessed be!*

Take a few deep breaths and gaze at the candle flame. Become aware of the changes in the atmosphere around you and the presence of the twelve signs.

Altar Work

Pick up the printout of your birth chart and look at your chart. Touch each of the twelve houses with your finger and push energy into them. You are energizing and awakening your birth chart to act as a focal point of power on the altar. Put your chart back on the altar when it feels ready to you. Then take the pad and pen and write the glyph for Aries again and again. The glyphs can be different sizes, they can overlap; you can make any pattern with them you like so long as you pour energy into the ink as you write. Scribing the glyph is an action that helps draw the interest of the spirit of Aries. Periodically look at the candle flame as you continue scribing the glyph. When you feel sensations in your body such as electric tingles, warmth, shivers, or something that you associate with the approach of a spirit, it is time to move on to the next step. If these are new experiences for you, just follow your instincts. Put away the pen and paper and pick up the sheet with the invocation of Aries.

Invoking Aries

Before beginning, think on what you hope to accomplish in this ritual and why it matters to you. Then speak these lines slowly and with conviction.

> *Aries, hear me, for I am born in the roar of the cardinal fire.*
> *Aries, see me, for the Aries Sun shines upon me.*
> *Aries, know me as a member of your family and your company.*
> *Aries, know me as your student and your protégé.*
> *Aries, know me as a conduit for your power.*
> *Aries, know me as a wielder of your magick.*
> *I am of you, and you are of me.*
> *I am of you, and you are of me.*
> *I am of you, and you are of me.*
> *Aries is here, within and without.*
> *Blessed be!*

Your Requests

Now, look at the candle for several deep breaths, and silently or aloud welcome the spirit of Aries. Close your eyes and ask for any guidance that would be beneficial for you and listen. It may take some time before anything comes through, so be patient. I find it valuable to receive guidance before making a request so that I can refine or modify intentions and outcomes. Consider the meaning of whatever impressions or guidance you received and reaffirm your intentions and desired outcomes for this ritual.

It is more effective to use multiple modes of communication to make your request. Speak silently or aloud the words that describe your need and how it could be solved. Visualize the same message but without the words and project the images on your mind's screen. Then put all your attention on your feelings and your bodily sensations that have been stirred up by contemplating your appeal to the spirit of Aries. Once again, wait and use all your physical and psychic senses to perceive what is given. At this point in the ritual, if there are objects to be charged, touch them or focus your gaze on them.

Offer Gratitude

You may be certain or uncertain about the success of the ritual or the time frame for the outcomes to become clear. Regardless of that, it is a good practice to offer thanks and gratitude to the spirit of Aries for being present. Also, thank yourself for doing your part of the work. The state of heart and mind that comes with thanks and gratitude makes it easier for the work to become manifest. Thanks and gratitude also act as a buffer against the unintended consequences that can be put into motion by rituals.

Release the Ritual

If you are seated, stand if you are able and face the east. Slowly turn clockwise until you come full circle while repeating the following or something similar.

> *Return, return oh turning wheel to your*
> *starry home*
> *Farewell, farewell oh Aries bright until we*
> *speak again.*

Another option while saying these words is to hold your hand over your head and trace a clockwise circle of the zodiac with your finger. When you are done, snuff out the candle on the altar and say,

> *It is done. It is done. It is done.*

Afterward

I encourage you to write down your thoughts and observations of what you experienced in the ritual. Do this while it is still fresh in mind before the details begin to blur. The information will become more useful over time as you work more with the spirit of Aries. It will also let you evaluate the outcomes of your workings and improve your process in future workings. This note-taking or journaling will also help you dial in any changes or refinements to this ritual for future use. Contingent upon the guidance you received or the outcomes you desire, you may want to add reminders to your calendar.

More Options

These are some modifications to this ritual that you may wish to try:

+ Put together or purchase Aries incense to burn during the ritual. An Aries oil to anoint the candle is another possibility. I'm providing one of my oil recipes as a possibility.

+ Set up a richer and deeper altar. In addition to adding more objects that resonate to the energy of Aries or Mars, consecrate each object before the ritual. You may also want to place an altar cloth on the table that brings to mind Aries, Mars, or the element of fire.

+ Creating a sigil to concentrate the essence of what you are working toward would be a good addition to the altar.

+ Consider adding chanting, free-form toning, or movement to raise energy for the altar work and/or for invoking Aries.

+ If you feel inspired, you can write your own invocations for the calling the zodiac and/or invoking Aries. This is a great way to deepen your understanding of the signs and to personalize your ritual.

Rituals have greater personal meaning and effectiveness when you personalize them and make them your own.

ARIES ANOINTING OIL RECIPE

***

Ivo Dominguez, Jr.

This oil is used for charging and consecrating candles, crystals, and other objects you use in your practice. This oil makes it easier for an object to be imbued with Aries energy. It also primes and tunes the objects so your will and power as an Aries witch flows more easily into it. Do not apply the oil to your skin unless you have done an allergy test first.

Ingredients:

- Carrier oil—1 ounce
- Frankincense—5 drops
- Basil—6 drops
- Peppermint—4 drops
- Dragon's Blood—2 drops
- Bergamot—4 drops

Instructions:

Pour one ounce of a carrier oil into a small bottle or vial. The preferred carrier oils are almond oil or fractionated coconut oil, but others can be used. Ideally use essential oils, but fragrance oils can be used as substitutes. Add the drops of the essential oils into the carrier oil. Once they have all been added, cap the bottle tightly, and shake the bottle several times. Hold the bottle in your hands, take a breath, and pour energy into the oil. Visualize red energy, the glyph for Aries, repeat the word *Aries*, and raise energy in your preferred manner. Continue doing so until the oil feels warm, seems to glow, or you sense that it is charged.

Label the bottle and store the oil in a cool, dark place. Consider keeping a little bit of each previous batch of oil to add to the new batch. This helps build the strength and continuity of the energy and intentions you have placed in the oil. Over time, that link makes your oils more powerful.

BETTER EVERY DAY: THE WAY FORWARD

Diotima Mantineia

The craft of the witch is a lifelong journey of learning and practice. It's a path of connecting with the world around us on subtle, magical levels. Drawing energy from those levels allows us to play with reality, to bend and shape it in cocreative ways, to become the artist of our life.

And as any artist will tell you, art demands constant vigilance—a committed engagement with both physical and spiritual realities.

With the plethora of information on all the many branches of witchcraft that is available to us, it can be difficult to decide how to structure a magical and spiritual practice that will support us and help us become better artists, better witches, and better humans.

Many years of working with astrology clients have confirmed for me what I learned early on in my studies: Sun is always at the heart of a chart, and we are meant to actively engage with our Sun sign to steer our life's journey. For an Aries witch, this involves working with the Warrior archetype.

Engaging the Warrior

About two years after I opened my magical bookstore, a kung fu school moved into the storefront next to mine. I started taking classes there and, for me, it was life changing. Learning this ancient Chinese martial art redefined my relationship with my body and the world around me. But mostly, it changed my understanding of the archetype of the Warrior and gave me a deeper appreciation of the philosophy behind it—a philosophy that is well suited to helping the Aries witch make the most of their natural abilities.

I had known for years that the Warrior was an essential archetype for Aries—after all, the sign itself was named after Ares, the Greek god of war, and Mars, Aries' ruling planet, was named after the Roman god of war. But, as a woman, I had never been particularly comfortable with that association. The culture of the 1950s and 60s that I was raised in frowned on assertive women—men were supposed to do the fighting for us. So, there was no model for women learning to fight, except for Wonder Woman, who was, after all, a comic book character.

Additionally, I was a peace-and-love flower child—a firm believer in the then-popular (and still true) bumper sticker axiom "War is not healthy for children and other living things." I marched for peace, then went to yoga classes where I chanted and meditated for inner peace.

But, like so many others of my generation, both current and personal events brought me to the realization that peace is something that must be defended. What we love is what we are willing to take a stand for. What we will defend. That defense does not necessarily require taking up arms. What it does require is the skill, discipline, and philosophy of the Warrior.

Everyone has the sign Aries in their chart. Everyone has at least a little bit of the Warrior energy in them. But for an Aries Sun, it is a central part of our Self. We cannot ignore or suppress it. If we don't pursue and integrate the positive attributes, the power and vision of the Warrior, we become more likely to live out its negative aspects, because it is at the heart of who we are.

The Warrior protects what they value, welcomes and steps up to a challenge, and is willing to fight for what they believe is right. But if they are driven by a need for power untethered from deeply held personal values and spiritual reality, that's when we see the shadow side, which encompasses everything from the horrors of war, colonialism, and wanton destruction of entire cultures to bullying and outbursts of rage.

It's important for Aries, and particularly Aries witches, to consciously develop the Warrior archetype within them. First, it's a built-in source of magical power for us—one we can access easily, because it resonates with our natal Sun. But also, because the witch often finds themselves needing to stand up to others, to defend those who need defending, to set protective boundaries. Witches often find themselves working to destroy injustice, corruption, and webs of negativity that hold people back from being able to improve their lives.

A warrior does not require physical strength or fighting skills, though quite a few choose to develop those skills. Magic is a witch's weapon, and any witch can choose to develop their skills as a warrior. Here are some thoughts on how an Aries witch can develop their natural skills and step into the archetype of the Warrior.

Self-Discipline

I've been known to joke that my only really solid daily practice is my morning cup of coffee, and I even skip that sometimes. You may find daily practice hard to keep up with, too, since Aries are easily bored, and not big fans of constant repetition. But developing and maintaining skills demands repetition and commitment to a path of self-improvement. Aries people may not be fans of repetition, but we have a strong will that allows us to power through boredom in pursuit of the accomplishments regular practice can bring.

It takes practice to develop the skills we need to embody the Warrior. Those skills include situational awareness, knowledge of and competency with whatever your weapons of choice are, and quick, but accurate, perception of and responses to threats. (Keep in mind that these threats are not solely physical. Neither are the weapons. Life is full of intangible threats like emotional manipulation, backstabbing acquaintances, gossip, and hostile psychic energies, not to mention our own subconscious urges toward self-sabotage, and we can use magic to defend ourselves against them.)

Certain physical, magical, spiritual, and energetic techniques, practiced regularly, bring us strength, skills, insight, clarity, and increasing magical power, but it takes discipline to do this work. Fortunately, discipline is something that can be developed, and there's more than one way to do that.

The "just grit your teeth and do it" approach works for many folks. But I would caution that this path can lead to psychological and emotional repression as well as spiritual bypassing. Putting our entire focus on an external conformity to rules—even if they are rules we made up for ourselves—can allow us to shut down and ignore real emotional, psychological, and/or spiritual wounds that need to be healed.

Ideally, self-discipline is grounded in self-knowledge and a desire for personal and spiritual growth. Discipline fueled by desire is a very different thing than discipline fueled by fear of consequences or sheer determination. To get there, we need to find, face, and release the fears that are holding us back. If the demands of training and practices seem too difficult to keep up with, then it may be time to reassess those practices. It may help to work with a therapist or mentor to remove the fears and spark a real desire to do the necessary work to follow your chosen path.

Living by Our Core Values

A warrior witch also requires a well-articulated and closely held set of core values. Getting very clear about our values helps us determine if we are using our Warrior skills in a way that is fully in line with our ethical principles.

Discovering those values is a journey, not a weekend workshop. When we get down to our bedrock core values, they are unchanging. But our journey often leads us to realize that what we thought were core values, aren't. They are values that were imprinted on us as children or that we took on when we were trying to fit in to a group. So, it's important to regularly revisit and question our values to make sure they are holding steady in the face of our life experiences, and make sure we are living our lives in line with those values. I find the introspective dark of the new Moon and the revealing light of the full Moon to be good check-in points for this work. After setting up ritual space and invoking the deities and helping spirits I work with, I either make a fresh list of my core values or review a list I've previously made. Then I bring to mind some of the most memorable events of the past two weeks and consider whether I acted in line with my values in those situations. Sometimes, I make a little talisman to help me keep my life choices in line with my values.

Courage

Courage is another essential attribute of a Warrior witch. Everyone has some level of courage—we all take occasional risks and find that we have to face our fears. But risk-taking is not the same as courage. Courage means acting when we are genuinely afraid of at least one possible outcome of that action. It means facing our fears head-on and doing what needs to be done in spite of them.

We grow in courage every time we make the choice to do what is right and accept the consequences of our actions. The more we act with courage, the more we strengthen our faith in our ability to handle whatever life tosses our way, to act with skill and insight.

The Warrior archetype is an important one for the Aries witch to explore and integrate. What makes a warrior is skill, courage, determination, and a willingness to engage in conflict in service to their ideals and their community. An Aries witch has what it takes to become the highest manifestation of the Warrior archetype.

CONCLUSION

Ivo Dominguez, Jr.

I hope you are putting what you discovered in this book to use in your witchcraft. You may have a desire to learn more about how astrology and witchcraft fit together. One of the best ways to do this is to talk about it with other practitioners. Look for online discussions, and if there is a local metaphysical shop, check to see if they have classes or discussion groups. If you don't find what you need, consider creating a study group. Learning more about your own birth chart is also an excellent next step. Some resources for study are listed in the back of this book.

At some point, you may wish to call upon the services of an astrologer to give you a reading that is fine-tuned to your chart. There are services that provide not just charts but full chart readings that are generated by software. These are a decent tool and more economical than a professional astrologer, but they lack the finesse and intuition that only a person can offer. Nonetheless, they can be a good starting point. If you do decide to hire an astrologer to do your chart, shop around to find someone attuned to your spiritual needs. You may decide to learn enough astrology to read your own chart, and that will serve you for many reasons. However, for the same reasons that tarot readers will go to someone else for a reading, the same is true with astrological readers. It is hard to see some things when you are too attached to the outcomes.

If you find your interest in astrology and its effect on a person's relationship to witchcraft has been stimulated by this book, you may wish to read the other books in this series. Additionally, if you have other witches that you work with, you'll find that knowing more about how they approach their craft will make your collective efforts more productive. Understanding them better will also help reduce conflicts or misunderstandings. The ending of this book is really the beginning of the adventure.

APPENDIX
ARIES CORRESPONDENCES

March 21–April 20

Symbol: ♈

Solar System: Mars, Sun

Seasons: Spring, Summer

Day: Tuesday

Celebration: Spring Equinox

Runes: Ehwaz, Feoh

Element: Fire

Colors: Pink, Red, White, Yellow

Energy: Yang

Chakras: Root, Solar Plexus, Brow

Number: 1

Tarot: Emperor

Trees: Alder, Blackthorn, Cedar, Cherry, Fir, Hawthorn, Holly, Juniper, Locust, Olive, Palm (Dragon's Blood), Pine, Willow

Herb and Garden: Anemone, Angelica, Basil, Blackberry/Bramble, Broom, Carnation, Dandelion, Fennel, Garlic, Geranium, Gorse, Honeysuckle, Marjoram, Peppermint, Rosemary, Thyme

Miscellaneous Plants: Allspice, Betony, Blessed Thistle, Cinnamon, Clove, Coriander, Cowslip, Cumin, Deer's Tongue, Frankincense, Galangal, Ginger, Mustard, Nettle, Pepper

Gemstones and Minerals: Agate (Fire), Apache Tears, Aquamarine, Aventurine, Bloodstone, Carnelian, Citrine, Diamond, Emerald, Garnet, Hematite, Herkimer Diamond, Jade, Jasper (Red), Lapis Lazuli, Opal (Fire), Quartz (Clear), Ruby, Sard, Sardonyx, Spinel

Metals: Gold, Iron, Steel

From the Sea: Coral

Goddesses: Anat, Badb, Cybele, Durga, Hecate, Hestia, Ishtar, Macha, Minerva, the Morrigan, Sekhmet, Tiamat

Gods: Amun, Ares, Belenus, Indra, Khnum, Marduk, Mars, Nergal, Ra

Angel: Michael

Animals: Goat, Sheep (Ram)

Birds: Hawk (Red-Tailed), Magpie, Owl, Robin, Woodpecker

Issues, Intentions, and Powers: Action, Ambition, Anger, Assertiveness, Beginnings, Business, Confidence, Courage, Desire, Emotions, Energy, Fear, Growth, Independence, Jealousy, Leadership, Life (Vitality), Light, Lust, Needs, Obstacles, Optimism, Passion, Pleasure, Pregnancy/Childbirth, Sexuality (Virility), Warmth

Excerpted with permission from *Llewellyn's Complete Book of Correspondences: A Comprehensive & Cross-Referenced Resource for Pagans & Wiccans* © 2013 by Sandra Kynes.

RESOURCES

Online

Astrodienst: Free birth charts and many resources.
- https://www.astro.com/horoscope

Astrolabe: Free birth chart and software resources.
- https://alabe.com

The Astrology Podcast: A weekly podcast hosted by professional astrologer Chris Brennan.
- https://theastrologypodcast.com

Magazine

The world's most recognized astrology magazine (available in print and digital formats).
- https://mountainastrologer.com

Books

- *Practical Astrology for Witches and Pagans* by Ivo Dominguez, Jr.
- *Parkers' Astrology: The Definitive Guide to Using Astrology in Every Aspect of Your Life* by Julia and Derek Parker

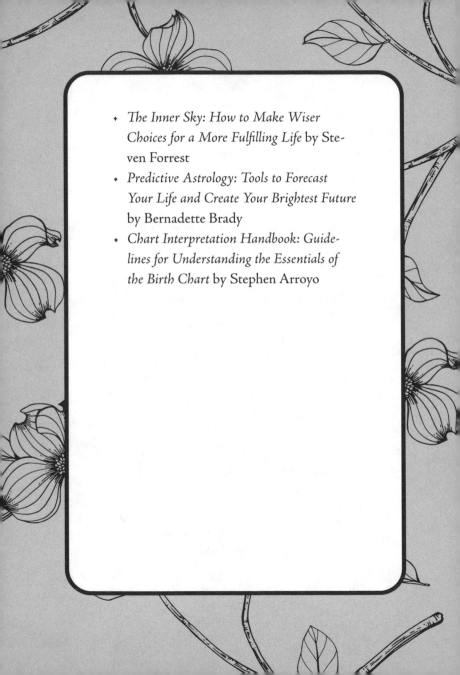

CONTRIBUTORS

We give thanks and appreciation to all our guest authors who contributed their own special Aries energy to this project.

Danielle Blackwood

Danielle Blackwood (Salt Spring Island, British Columbia) is a professional astrologer with more than thirty years of experience, as well as a Registered Counseling Therapist (RTC) in private practice. She is the author of *The Twelve Faces of the Goddess* and *A Lantern in the Dark*. Visit her at https://danielleblackwood.com/.

Michael Cabrera

Michael Cabrera is a Feri initiate and a Minos in the Minoan Brotherhood tradition. He is the author of the Pagan fiction novel *The Wheel and the Day*. He currently lives in the Washington, DC, metropolitan area.

Cat Castells

Cat Castells is a Third Degree High Priestess and Elder of the Blue Star Tradition of Wicca. She is also a graphic artist, owns two retail stores, and makes cool stuff on her laser. In her copious spare time from all of that, she loves birding, movies, and reading.

Jack Chanek

Jack Chanek is a Gardnerian Wiccan and tarot reader who has been working with the cards since he was eleven years old. He has taught workshops on tarot, Qabalah, and Wicca around the country and is the author of *Qabalah for Wiccans* and *Tarot for Real Life*. He lives in New Jersey, where he works as an academic philosopher. Visit him at www.JackOf WandsTarot.wordpress.com.

Lilith Dorsey

Lilith Dorsey (New Orleans, LA) comes from a background of Celtic, Afro-Caribbean, and Native American spirituality. They have long been committed to providing accurate and respectful information about the African Traditional Religions and are proud to be a published Black author of such titles as *The African-American Ritual Cookbook*; *Orishas, Goddesses and Voodoo Queens*; *Water Magic*; and the newly rereleased *Voodoo and African Traditional Religion*. Visit them at https://lilith dorsey.com/.

Dawn Aurora Hunt

Dawn Aurora Hunt, owner of Cucina Aurora Kitchen Witchery, is the author of *A Kitchen Witch's Guide to Love & Romance* and *Kitchen Witchcraft for Beginners*. Though not born under the sign of Aries, she combines knowledge of spiritual goals and magickal ingredients to create recipes for all Sun signs in this series. She is a Scorpio. Find her at www.CucinaAurora.com.

Sandra Kynes

Sandra Kynes (Midcoast Maine) is the author of nineteen books, including *Mixing Essential Oils for Magic*, *Magical Symbols and Alphabets*, *Crystal Magic*, *Plant Magic*, and *Sea Magic*. Excerpted content from her book, *Llewellyn's Complete Book of Correspondences*, has been used throughout this series. She is a Scorpio. Find her at http://www.kynes.net.

Crow Walker

Crow Walker makes her home in the Pacific Northwest with cats, harps, and too many books to count. She is an initiate in the Anderson Feri and Reclaiming traditions of the Craft and believes that with great power comes great responsibility to use that power for the good of all.

Notes

Notes

Notes

To Write to the Author

If you wish to contact the author or would like more information about this book, please write to the author in care of Llewellyn Worldwide Ltd. and we will forward your request. Both the author and the publisher appreciate hearing from you and learning of your enjoyment of this book and how it has helped you. Llewellyn Worldwide Ltd. cannot guarantee that every letter written to the author can be answered, but all will be forwarded. Please write to:

Ivo Dominguez, Jr.
Diotima Mantineia
℅ Llewellyn Worldwide
2143 Wooddale Drive
Woodbury, MN 55125-2989

Please enclose a self-addressed stamped envelope for reply,
or $1.00 to cover costs. If outside the U.S.A., enclose
an international postal reply coupon.

Many of Llewellyn's authors have websites with additional information and resources. For more information, please visit our website at:

www.llewellyn.com